MW01640324

Two Epistles of St. Patrick the Bishop

Translated by Patricia Colling Egan
with Introductions and Notes

St. Nicholas Press
Maysville, Missouri

First Edition 2021

St. Nicholas Press is an imprint of the Road to Emmaus Foundation.
Publications may be purchased in quantity for educational, business
or promotional use. For ordering information write or call:

St. Nicholas Press/Road to Emmaus Foundation
PO Box 198
Maysville, MO 64469

Phone and Fax: (+1) 816-449-5231
Email: stnicholaspress@gmail.com
roadtoemmausfoundation@gmail.com

Visit our websites at:
www.roadtoemmaus.net
www.stnicholaspress.net

ISBN: 978-1-63551-101-7
Library of Congress Control Number: 9781635511017

Printed in China

The image of Eadwine, the 12th-century scribe opposite Scribe's Poem,
is both used with permission of Alamy Stock photos. The rendering of
verses from the "Lorica" of St. Patrick is based on a 19th-century version
of it in C. F. Alexander's "Saint Patrick's Breastplate." Other poems are
the author's versions of anonymous poetry from the Middle Ages.

Layout and Cover: Bruce Petersen Art Direction & Design

SRIPTORVM PRINCEPS EGO NEC OBITURA DEINCEPS LAVS MEA NEC FAMA QVIS
SIM MEA LITTERA CLAMA · LITTERA TE TVA SRIPTVRA QVEM SIGNAT PICTA FIGVRA
PREDICAT EADWINVM FAMA PER SECVLA VIVVM · INGENIVM CVIVS LIBRI DECVS IND
CAT HVIVS · QVEM TIBI SEQVE DATVM MVNVS DEVS ACCIPE GRATVM

My hand aches with writing,
unsteady, my craft's sharp tool;
its slender beak spewing bright ink,
a beetle-dark, shining draught.

The God of Light's streams of wisdom
flow from my narrow, tanned hand
flooding the page with splashes
of green-leafed holly ink.

My dribbly little pen scratches
across a vast white vellum plain,
its treasure-strewn path, unending;
thus my aching hand.

After an 11th-century scribe's poem[i]

TABLE OF CONTENTS

Scribe's Poem i

Before Saint Patrick iv

Map vi

Apologia vii

I

Confessio of Patricius the Bishop 1

II

Preface to *Pastoral Epistle* 25

Pastoral Epistle 31

III

Excerpt from the *Lorica* 38

Chronology 39

Endnotes 41

Select References 73

Before Saint Patrick[x]

I

I summon Eireann:
oft-sailed fertile seas
fertile fruitful mountains
fruitful showery woods
showers falling in rivers
falls springing from lakes
springs pooling on the hilltop
pooling men at Tara
Tara, hill of tribes
tribes of the sons of Mil.

FROM THE *INVOCATION OF AMERGIN*

II

High stood he here
grim image of cruel conflict:
Cromm Cruaich
reigning idol,
Eireann's Moloch
mist-wreathed, raddled heap
overlooking fields
oblivious of the eternal kingdom.

Round him in a circle stood
twelve stone idols
of the bitterly enslaved.
On Samhain's Eve
when seen and unseen worlds collide,
he glittered
surrounded by subjects,
blood-crusted, insatiable.

Wailing and fearful,
to him they offer their firstborn,
pouring new blood on the humped one.
In his shadow
they scream and mutilate their bodies.
For such worship
its name is Plain of Adoration:
Magh Slecht.
From Eremon's reign,
that noble, graceful Goidel,
homage to such rocks was paid
till the coming of holy Patrick in Armagh.

AFTER A SIXTH-CENTURY POEM: *MAGH SLECHT*

Significant Places in Patrick's World

Apologia

A new rendering of an oft-translated work demands justification for its existence in a way required of no other literary effort. And, in the case of the letters of St. Patrick, some may wonder what could be so compelling about re-presenting writings of a man who lived a thousand years before Columbus? What do they matter *now*? For the present, let's just assume that they do, or at least grant that this writer was convinced enough of their importance to us that she spent decades poring over them.[ii]

The present work was undertaken because, when I began to write a book dealing with the unresolved mysteries of St. Patrick's life (e.g. his homeland, his ethnicity, his "trial"), no existing translation of his writings served my purposes. I was looking for clarity and a rendering of his letters that could be easily digested by an English-speaking public. Only with such a tool could one work with these most fundamental texts for the unraveling of the Patrician mysteries[1]. I realized then that I would have to make a new translation myself, however absurd or presumptiuous the attempt might appear.

The contribution this translation hopes to make lies primarily in clarifications of words and meanings at critical places in the epistles where previous renderings have fallen short of understanding or coherence.

Moderns may rephrase one of the previous questions: "Why do these epistles need unraveling? Who cares what a fifth-century bishop in Ireland – or anywhere else – thought or did?" If one considers that the self-understanding of a nation rests on events in the long ago past, one will see the necessity of describing those events as accurately as is humanly possible. And, when that long ago past has been distorted by misperceptions, national self-understanding is similarly distorted and history misconstrued.

For over fifteen hundred years there have been significant misperceptions engendered by the transmission of St. Patrick's life and writings and, because histories of fifth-century Britain have relied so heavily on what St. Patrick had to say, in the absence of other fifth-century sources and under the assumption that he came from Britain, I believe that unraveling confusions about the saint's life will result in a more accurate presentation of early British history and of early Church history in northwestern Europe.[iii]

1 References to the *Confessio* are abbreviated *Conf.* and to the *Pastoral Epistle* as *Epist.* The Latin edition of both epistles is readily available in David R. Howlett, *The Book of Letters of Saint Patrick the Bishop* (Dublin: Four Courts Press, 1996) or Ludwig Bieler, *Libri Epistolarum Sancti Patricii Episcopi* (Dublin: The Royal Irish Academy, 1993). Online see https://www.confessio.ie.

As for Ireland, it goes without saying that a truer picture of St. Patrick and his times will result in a clearer view of Ireland's birth as a Christian nation and of the man most responsible for its transformation.

Encountering the mind and heart of a fifth-century person who knows how to express them has merit in itself. We discover how kin we are despite the lapse of centuries and we savor the perspective he brings to us from his own era. But what a remarkable treasure we have when the person in question was kidnapped from his luxurious Roman home in Gaul to become a slave in Ireland! This is the only voice of a fifth-century former slave able to reach us directly despite the cultural thickets separating us from him.

Patrick's first person accounts of his background, kidnapping, life as a slave in a foreign country, his escape and subsequent re-emergence as a Christian bishop have an energy and immediacy that renders intervening centuries irrelevant. And his interior consciousness of the workings of the Holy Spirit is an important early contribution to literature on Christian transformation, or *theosis*, as the East calls the phenomenon, still valid today.

Because much of what scholars have thought they knew about St. Patrick rested on erroneous conjectures of previous chroniclers whose times and cultures framed those conjectures without sufficient assistance from facts, it is essential to base any study of the saint on his own writings. Whatever contradicts them in subsequent biographies or fanciful hagiography should be rejected in favor of information supplied by the man himself – so long as one has no reason to question his veracity, something that has never been in doubt.

Translating his writings as well as possible to truly convey his meaning is fundamental to such study.

> It would be impertinent to try to rescue the works of Patrick from the state into which traditions of misdirected and acrimonious modern scholarship have brought them unless the Apostle of the Irish had provided the means. By listening to him on his own terms we can hear him speak articulately, authoritatively, compellingly, across fifteen centuries, with a power he believed to be not his own but God's.[2]

That Patrick speaks "articulately, authoritatively, compellingly" is news to many readers of his epistles. Content to imagine him as a rather dear but bumbling saint whose efforts at written communication verge on incoherence, many have missed the fact that he actually supplies us with everything necessary in order to know him and understand his life. And he does so with

2 Howlett, *op. cit.* 13.

a simple economy that is anything but artless. This translation aims to act as *defensor*[3] for the saint on trial before the Academy and the court of public opinion.

Patrick himself provides us with the judicial setting, thematically weaving ideas of judgment and law throughout the *Confessio*; the whole having been structured and conceived as a court, albeit a semi-eschatological one. In this court, Patrick acts as his own advocate supplying us with history and background germane to the case; contrasting his adherence to truth with awareness of the eternal consequences of lying. He adds to his veracity by the fact that, until his silence threatened God's work in Ireland, he kept the secrets of his episcopal hearing despite awareness of slanderous rumors damaging his personal reputation.

The courtroom drama takes center stage in Patrick's composition, followed by a long series of proofs illustrating the success of his ministry, his purity of intention regarding it, his fidelity to the task. Patrick initiates the last section, by saying: *Behold, I call on God as witness that I do not lie concerning my life,* and his final summing up begins: *I testify,* concluding with: *This is my testimony*[4] [before the invisible tribunal] *before I die.*

If defending Patrick before the courts of the Academy and public opinion is the historical/academic justification for this work, more important reasons have to do with spiritual, and thus deeply human, values that can enrich each of us as persons. The man who wrote these two letters is so extraordinary that truly knowing him cannot but ennoble and encourage us.

Furthermore, Patrick flourished in the fifth century as a member of the "one, holy, catholic and apostolic Church" centuries before diverging theologies, cultures, and events definitively split the faithful into East and West. Not only is he a window into the orthodox faith of the period, Patrick is a saint whom both East and West revere, a personality capable of helping to heal the Body of Christ of the wounds that mutilate it.

And he is timely. Faced with the unimaginable crumbling of the Western Roman Empire in his lifetime, Patrick did what all Christians need to do. He navigated his uncertain era with eyes on Christ and the Kingdom of God. The truth is that humans always live in crumbling times because the world, like time, is always passing away as we travel through it. They are blessed who, like Patrick, walk on the waters of the world refusing to allow temporal

3 A *defensor* was a defense lawyer, either secular or ecclesiastic, in a Roman legal proceeding. Ecclesiastical *defensors* were specially trained deacons who served the Church in its trials and hearings.

4 *Confessio* is the word here translated as *witness to God* because, in English, contextual realities alter the way the word "confession" is received. In Christian Latin, *confessio* refers to one's witness to God, one's testimony, and in this case, to the saint's life as witness to God's activity in it.

considerations to mesmerize them into sinking, keeping their focus on Christ and the establishment of a Kingdom that will not pass away.

A translator coming after so many centuries of other scholars' harrowing the same fields owes an immense debt to all her predecessors and could never have attempted the current work without standing on their shoulders. Special thanks go to St. Ultan of Ardbreccan, Tirechan, Muirchu moccu Mactheni, St. Fursa (who brought copies of the epistles to France in the seventh century, providing a basis for their printing in the seventeenth), Probus of Slane, Geoffrey Keating, Michel-Francois Dubuisson, Sir James Ware, the Bollandists, Jacques Malbrancq, S.J., Rev. William Canon Fleming, Rev. Dr. John Lanigan, Professor John Bagnell Bury, Professor Eoin MacNeill, Professor Ludwig Bieler, Dr. Christine Mohrmann, and Dr. David R. Howlett.

Armed with Professor Bieler's critical Latin edition of St. Patrick's letters, I began to wrestle with words mistranslated by previous scholars or which seemed to make no sense in context, pummeling phrases in an attempt to render Patrick's thought more comprehensible in English.[5] Because I suspected that the opacity of some words or phrases was due to erroneous choices of meanings, I set out to discover as old and extensive a Latin dictionary as possible in case more recent lexicons had, for the sake of economy, disposed of alternate meanings or ones more prevalent in the Late Roman Empire.

How fortunate that Barrie Pryble's "ABCD Bookstore" was then still in existence in nearby Camden, Maine! With her help I acquired the indispensable "enlarged and improved edition" of *A New and Copious Lexicon of the Latin Language; compiled chiefly from the Magnum Totius Latinitas Lexicon of Facciolati and Forellini, and the German works of Scheller and Luenemann* edited by F.P. Leverett. Published in Boston in 1853, this was a "new" edition of 1,342 pages, each having three columns of microscopic print describing the classical meanings of Latin words. The volume also includes the etymological index of Freund's lexicon as well as an English-Latin lexicon at the end.

By using this dictionary (now in pieces from constant consultation) with the support of other dictionaries, Bennett's *Latin Grammar* and Souter's *A Glossary of Later Latin,* and by comparing my efforts with those of other translators, I was able to arrive at a text that could provide a point of departure for the book I had originally planned to write. It occurred to me later that this translation, with its supplementary material, might be welcomed by others who, for various reasons, wished to better know and study St. Patrick.

5 See Bieler, *op. cit.* for a reconstruction of the history of the Patrician texts that absolves the saint of blame for errors committed by copyists over the centuries. Also see Howlett, *op. cit.* 40-46 for an idea of the way the saint's construction of his texts, if understood, insures correct transmission; or, if incorrectly transmitted, can reconstruct them.

Challenges presented by Patrician manuscripts are not limited to antiquity of language, structural peculiarities, or even to the complication of their author's having spent decades thinking and speaking a *Goidelic*[iv] form of Celtic in Ireland. The eight surviving Patrician manuscripts have suffered the "slings and arrows" of copyists, travel under difficult conditions, anacoluthic[6] biblical quotations, and less than optimal storage over the centuries. Of these, copyists have caused the most trouble.

Medieval Irish scribes did not necessarily understand either Latin or the content of what they transcribed. On occasion they have, with the best of intentions, "corrected" something on the basis of what they *did* understand, or under the influence of traditions composed of scraps of partially digested information. To arrive at a Latin text on which later scholars could rely was the great achievement of Professor Ludwig Bieler.

Saint Patrick wrote both of his surviving letters in a colloquial Latin he had not spoken much for years, except perhaps to his fellow Gallo-Roman clerics in Ireland. Immersed in the Irish language for decades, he was conscious of the "rusticity" of his native tongue made even more evident in light of the erudition of some to whom his thoughts were now being addressed. He refers to this rusticity several times, seeming to write disparagingly of his own skill.

Some have been misled by such humble remarks into assuming a lack of literary sophistication in the saint, which error Dr. David Howlett puts to rest with his *The Book of Letters of Saint Patrick the Bishop*. What has been generally overlooked is that confessing one's "rusticity" was a convention employed by even the most erudite among the Gallic literati, particularly those from the North who always acknowledged the linguistic refinements of their southern compatriots, so much closer to Rome and its culture. Like acknowledging oneself as a sinner before the ineffable perfection of God, humility before the literate community was commonly expressed to indicate an author's awareness of the high standards and literary sophistication of those who would read his work.

Dr. Howlett's perception that Patrick divided his *Confessio* into five sections corresponding to the first five books of the Hebrew Bible[7] is one with which I concur gratefully, because this recognition is a major tool for comprehension of the epistle. Patrick's **Genesis** is about beginnings, earthly and divine. His **Exodus** mirrors the Hebrews' servitude in and escape from

6 *Anacoluthic* refers to syntactical shifts within a sentence as can happen when one unites quotations (e.g. from the Bible) that have different grammatical structures.

7 See Howlett, *op. cit.* 110 for more on the biblical models for the *Confessio*.

Egypt, and their wanderings in the desert with his slavery in and escape from Ireland, and his wanderings in Gaul and Britain.

His version of **Leviticus** is concerned with religious particulars: some legalities of his preparation for the episcopacy and the Irish mission, just as the original related the religio-legal preparation of the Hebrew people for the Promised Land and their life in it. The longest section of the *Confessio*, **Numbers**, recounts the saint's many labors, numbers of converts, and the temptations that assailed him, in order to illustrate the success of his mission numerically. **Deuteronomy** concludes Patrick's personal epic just as its prototype brings the Moses story to an end.

However valuable his revelation of the *Confessio's* Pentateuchal divisions,[v] it is Dr. Howlett's pointing out the chiastic structure[8] of the epistle that is most essential for our penetration of Patrick's mind and meanings. Once one perceives that the epistle is composed as a series of concentric circles rather than in a straight line of development, meaning, hitherto obscured, is revealed.

And we see that it is at the center of chiasms that we will find keys to unlock what had previously been mysterious. Only then do we begin to appreciate the function of parallel phrases arranged in rings framing key statements at their centers. And only then do we realize that we have just scratched the surface of these epistles.

Because Patrick was abducted at an age when, like other boys of his class, he had embarked on rhetorical studies,[9] he was painfully aware of this interruption to his education, a deficiency he was required to supply later when studying for the diaconate, if not before.[vi] At that time he was almost certainly the butt of many jokes since much that was familiar to his considerably younger classmates would have been, for him, initially unfamiliar and difficult.

As some of those students, now his clerical colleagues, are among the individuals to whom the *Confessio* was addressed, I imagine his tongue occasionally rested in his cheek when he contrasted their "erudition" with his "lack of polish." For, Dr. Howlett, followed by Dr. Maire de Paor, exposes the mathematical intricacy of Patrick's chiastic literary structure supporting the complexity of his thought and rhetorical skill.

The combination of Patrick's actual virtuosity, his structural complexity, and the biblical quotations so masterfully interwoven with his thought, has added to the difficulty of translating him well into an English both truly

8 *Ibid.* 94ff. for more on the chiastic structure of Patrick's epistles.

9 *Conf.* (10)

representative of him and capable of assimilation by moderns. It has also contributed to negative assessments of his literary skills.

Perhaps those skills would be better appreciated if we understood what he was attempting to accomplish. For, if a person sets out to build a church, it is senseless to criticize him for not building a skyscraper. Patrick's rhetorical abilities were honed and employed on behalf of those he hoped would become or remain citizens of the Kingdom of God. As such they would have been essentially those of an orator, a preacher, whose congregations were made up of people who did not read, but were trained to listen, whose culture was transmitted orally.

Like St. Patrick's, St. Gregory of Tours' idiosyncratic genre was criticised for not being what it was never intended to be, and like Patrick, Gregory expresses his awareness of his distance from Latin prose stylists with conventional humility:

> I fear that when I begin to write, since I am without learning in rhetoric and the art of grammar, the learned will say to me "Uncouth and ignorant man, what makes you think that this gives you a place among writers?"[10]

Gregory's great accomplishment was to fuse colloquial Latin with the literary so that he was understood by those with whom he wished to communicate.

> That only appears an exceptional and refreshing achievement to anyone who has had to plough through the verbose and obscure circumlocutions of "correct" literary Latin of the fourth or fifth centuries, which must have been quite divorced from ordinary speech, and indeed almost certainly not comprehensible to most people in Gaul.[11]

To compare St. Patrick's writings to a Sidonius Appollonaris, or other literary luminaries, criticising them for not being what they were never intended to be is not only unjust. It is to entirely miss the wonder and the gift of what they actually are.

10 Edward James, trans., *Gregory of Tours' Life of the Fathers* (Liverpool: Liverpool University Press, 1991) xviii.

11 *Ibid.* xix.

Since I was unable to display Patrick's chiastic structure in the text, or to indicate every biblical quote and still accomplish my purpose, I have attempted neither, only occasionally marking the latter with quotation marks where they clarify a sentence or are required for the sense of it.

At the time Patrick's letters were written, punctuation marks were not in use, so it has been left to translators to insert them. By virtue of a set of previously misplaced quotation marks, the major interpretive key to Patrick's self-defense against resurrected slanders from his pre-episcopal hearing was lost. It is easily retrieved when the marks are properly placed.

Passages, hitherto opaque, become transparent when an alternate meaning (available in the 1853 lexicon or in Souter's *A Glossary of Later Latin*) is substituted for a common translation. A case in point is the word *pupillus*, translated by other Patrician scholars as "pupil." While this is one rendering of the Latin, in antiquity the word was more generally used to mean "fatherless boy" or "orphan."

Even when it did mean "pupil" the Roman understanding of the word was not simply equivalent to our "student." "Pupil" implied the existence of a tutor, which in turn meant that the boy in question was without a father, for the Roman tutor was a guardian, a regent who looked after the affairs of his fatherless charge until the boy came of age at fourteen. Its use by Patrick to describe himself long after he could be considered a boy or under the care of a tutor tells us that he views himself as fatherless, or orphaned, one whose tutor was God and who is grateful for the guidance and care shown him by his heavenly Father in the absence of his earthly father, Calpurnius.

Manuscripts must have differed, perhaps due to a copier's error, as to whether the word *enim* or *enon* appears in the sentence about Patrick's family background. I have chosen *enon* because the Latin construction makes no sense if *enim* is used, leaving one with a dangling phrase and a *non sequitur*. *Enon* is an early reading found in the seventeenth-century edition of Sir James Ware, who studied the Patrician manuscripts when they must have been in better condition than they are now, and less conserved.

Damage to a manuscript, previous efforts to restore it, or fading could easily suggest that the questionable word was *enim*. Some early transcribers, knowledgeable enough to be aware that there is no *enon* in Latin, may even have substituted *enim* for the word they read, assured that previous scribes had copied a predecessor's calligraphy erroneously.[vii]

Subsequent research seemed to confirm my preference, revealing that the river near the Calpurnius estate, (now called the *Liane*) had been called *Fluvius Ennius* or *Fluvius Enna* by the Romans, and *En/Elne*, meaning "water," by the local Celtic inhabitants, the *Morini*. *Enon* would then be translated *En River* or *Water River, on/aun/aven* being a Celtic word for river.

According to Bullet's *Dictionnaire Celtique*, *enn*, as distinguished from *en*, meant habitation. Thus *Enon* could even have been a play on *en* and *enn* resulting in *Water House* or *River Dwelling*. They would be appropriate names for a property bordering a river, particularly one that, like the *En/Elne/Liane*, flooded seasonally, depositing alluvial riches on nearby meadows and fields, thus deepening the relationship between land and water.

These are just two examples illustrating ways in which this translation differs from others – ways which, one hopes, may serve to contribute to our understanding of the remarkable man who has inspired so much scholarship over so many centuries.

Translations also differ in style. We, who neither think in nor speak Latin, need a version of St. Patrick's epistles that will slide into our minds with the ease originals slid into the minds to which they were addressed. Because translators have widely divergent aims: some aiming at word for word accuracy; others, to reveal chiastic patterns or to demonstrate the frequency of biblical quotations; and still others, to reach particular audiences, they do not necessarily serve the general public at whom this effort is aimed.

Since my purpose is to allow as many as possible to "meet" St. Patrick, we begin with the *Confessio*, which probably preceded the *Pastoral Epistle*, although that has not been the prevailing opinion. Composed close to the end of his life and giving a broad overview of it, the *Confessio* provides a better foundation for beginning to know the saint than does his *Pastoral Epistle*, inspired by a brutal attack on newly baptised Christians and less furnished with the biographical information we are seeking.

Footnotes are included in the text and, to accommodate those with particular questions or of a more scholarly bent, there are also endnotes with supplementary material. The latter provide glimpses of early Ireland and Patrick's Gaul that add color and context to the epistles. In an effort to reduce the number of quotation marks, when I refer to excerpts from his epistles, they are reproduced in italics without quotation marks, except where the saint himself is quoting.

There are a few places where the text is indented or in boldface in order to reflect a change in the saint's narration. These appear at the center of each epistle where Patrick reveals the cause of the betrayals he relates; when he soars into prayer in the final sections of each letter; or, in one instance at a long parenthetical explanation. The reason for changes in type is to assist the narrative visually by separating a major revelation, a hymn-like prayer, or a lengthy explanatory detour from the surrounding account.[12]

This translation is made from Professor Bieler's Latin edition, only occasionally preferring variants from other manuscripts as, for example, choosing *enon* rather than *enim* in *Conf.* (1) or *carne* rather than *canes* in *Conf.* (19). In the notes direct quotes from Patrick's letters are referenced in parentheses to Bieler's commonly accepted chapter divisions.

A word about our saint's name: *Patricius*[viii] is the only name he uses to identify himself in his letters, but it was not given him at birth. In the fifth century, and until the eighth, when Pope Stephen II (III) usurped the emperor's prerogative in order to confer the patrician rank on Pepin the Short (helping to effect the western Church's shift from alliance with Byzantium to alliance with the Franks) *Patricius* was an honorific *agnomen* bestowed by an emperor in recognition of great accomplishment on behalf of the empire.[13]

Such a Patrician ranked next after a consul, who was himself just below an emperor. For anyone whose cultural background was Roman, or even exposed to *Romanitas*,[14] the name *Patricius* was a reminder of that rank and, in this case, a subtle reinforcement of episcopal authority. This is worth mentioning in order to point out that St. Patrick was considered extraordinary by his superiors and peers during his lifetime, not merely elevated to greatness after death by the admiration of the pagans he had converted. Both *Confessio* and *Pastoral Epistle* begin with *Ego Patricius* or *I, Patricius.*

Nor has veneration for the saint been limited to Ireland or fifth-century rulers and ecclesiastics. "Wherever the Scoto-Irish settled in G. Britain, there were churches erected under the name of St. Patrick; ex.c. in Argyle . . . . Several of the old churches in the Hebrides went under his name."[15] There was an ancient church dedicated to the saint on the Isle of Man and another ancient church, belonging to an Irish monastery at Glastonbury, existing at least from the seventh century and originally dedicated to the Blessed Virgin Mary and St. Patrick.

In the sixth century, St. Columbanus (who founded monasteries at Annegray, Luxeuil, Fontaine, and Bobbio) and many other Irish missionary monks planted religious houses in areas on the Continent where Patrick is still re-

12 This last occurs only once, in **Leviticus** to mark a long explanation, almost a flashback.

13 An *agnomen* was a fourth name added to the Roman *tria nomina* (triple name) to honor its bearer for some notable achievement. See *I, Patricius, op. cit.* Chapter VI.

14 *Romanitas* is a term expressing the complex of culture, laws and customs defining the Roman presence wherever it was experienced in the world.

15 Rev. John Lanigan, *D.D. An Ecclesiastical History of Ireland, Vol. I* (Dublin: Graisberry, 1822) 67, n. 53.

vered, like Wurtemburg in Germany or the Styrian part of Austria. We find the saint commemorated in early calendars, martyrologies, and breviaries throughout Europe.

The French paleographer, Dom Jean Mabillon, published seventh-century litanies[16] composed for the Celtic churches of Ireland, Scotland, Wales, and Cornwall, which he discovered in the library at Rheims. These featured St. Patrick and other Irish saints, although none who were English. Seventh-century Irish missionary monks brought their veneration of St. Patrick to Peronne[17] along with some secondary relics and copies of his letters.

And there are other indications that Patrick was revered in France even before the arrival of the Irish monks. Survivals of particular affection for the saint abound with place, family and church names memorializing him; ancient Patrician legends from many parts of northern France; in his inclusion in northern French martyrologies and breviaries; and the continued use of Patrice for masculine names.

During the twelfth century, relics of Sts. Peter and Paul, said to have been brought to Ireland by St. Patrick, along with relics of the saint himself, were deposited in the Cathedral of *Sens*, the first great Gothic cathedral, at that time the seat of the primate of Gaul. In periods of danger and unrest we find relics being translated to places of greater safety, thus the translation of twelfth-century relics may relate to the Norman conquest of Ireland or to danger from conflicts among the Irish themselves.

Also in the twelfth century, the Canons Regular of St. John Lateran in Rome,[18] motivated by their own deep respect and love for the saint, spread his cult even farther around western Europe. A relic of Patrick was brought to Fermo, Italy in the seventeenth century, almost certainly by Rinuccini, the papal nuncio who supported Catholic Ireland against Cromwell and who later became bishop of Fermo.

In Spain and Italy churches are named for the saint (e.g. *San Patrizio* in Ravenna; *Torre di San Patrizio* in Fermo, where there is also a well: *Pozzo di San Patrizio*) and baptismal registers where devotion to the saint was strong are full of *Patritios* and *Patricios*. After the people of Lorca, Spain ended

16 These litanies can be found in Mabillon's *Vetera Analecta, Tomi II* (Paris: F. Montalant, 1723) 669.

17 Saint Fursey, the Irish monk who brought St. Patrick's epistles and, according to some, his relics, to France in the seventh century, was buried at Peronne. Known as *Peronna Scottorum*, Peronne was founded by St. Fursey's brother, Foillan, and was a haven for Irish pilgrims.

18 Devotion to St. Patrick was still flourishing in the eighteenth century among the Lateran Canons of Padua who commissioned Tiepolo's altarpiece "The Miracle of St. Patrick."

nearly 600 years of Muslim domination, they built *Colegio San Patricio* in memory of the saint to whose intercession they attributed their victory.[19] [ix]

If modern times have reduced our saint to the stature of a nationalistic figurine, early centuries viewed him more universally with a reverence that ignored national boundaries. Heroes reflect a culture. Is ours elevated by the replacement of great saints with rock, sports and film stars? Or might we moderns benefit from a more discriminating array of heroes to remember and emulate? Surely Patricius, the "Enlightener of Ireland"[20] would appear prominently among the pool of candidates.

Profiting from light shed by Dr. David Howlett's painstaking work, I hope to dispel false ideas about Patrick's erudition and literary skill. How typical of us humans is the temptation to assume that others are lacking when it is we who have not managed to penetrate their meaning or perceive their skill!

For those whose curiosity is roused about conclusions to which I have come regarding disputed areas of Patrick's life, I refer you to the companion volume, *I, Patricius: The Roman History of an Irish Saint* which contains much more in the way of explanation and documentation.

Finally, a word about the title: *Two Epistles of St. Patrick the Bishop.* We are treating of the only two Patrician writings that have survived to us, but the original corpus probably included others; among them, perhaps, the letter referred to in Patrick's *Pastoral Epistle* which immediately preceded his formal response to the criminal attack on his newly baptised and chrismated Christians.

"Epistle" rather than "letter" has been chosen to describe them because these two works are both carefully constructed formal expressions of a bishop: the first to his fellow bishops and clerics in Gaul and Ireland and perhaps to the emperor; the second, to his Irish flock, its apostates, and its clergy.

Although the saint explains that he is sending the *Pastoral Epistle* to Coroticus and his mercenaries, the explanation is information he is imparting to his primary addressees, those whom he is able to affect by the kind of rhetoric he employs, the members of his church. But because apostates from his flock have thrown in their lot with Coroticus for gain, the only way Patrick can hope to reach them is by ensuring that Coroticus receives the epistle.

19 Tomas Cardinal O Fiaich, "Veneration of Saint Patrick in Italy and Spain" in *Seanchas Ard Mhacha: Journal of the Armagh Diocesan Historical Society, Vol. 4 No. 2* (Armagh: Cumann Seanchais Ard Mhacha, 1961) 101-103. One wonders whether relics reputed to have been deposited at Sens were a result of the translation of Patrick's remains at Downpatrick in the twelfth century.

20 This title is applied to the saint by the Orthodox Church.

Why were the epistles written? The *Confessio*, is a hymn of gratitude and praise to God for His loving care manifest in all the vicissitudes of the saint's life. But it probably would not have been written, or widely disseminated, unless he had been elevated to the rank of Patricius. Recirculated rumors from Patrick's episcopal hearing, revived by the amazing fact of his elevation, threatened to undermine Patrick's work in Ireland, prompting him to mount a defense of his life and work against the slanderous accusations.

At the center of the *Confessio*, in **Leviticus**, we find an account of that hearing, and of the saint's betrayal by his closest friend in the diaconate. It is followed by Part IV, **Numbers**, his defense against the particular offense with which he was charged, namely that he undertook the Irish mission in order to enrich himself.

The *Pastoral Epistle* is a response to worse treachery. Some of Patrick's flock had turned their backs on the faith and betrayed their newly baptised Christian brothers and sisters to Coroticus and his mercenaries for gain. The letter is addressed particularly to these apostates in hopes of their repentance, the return of the kidnapped women intended for sale in Britain, and restoration of the stolen goods. Those murdered were men.

Study of the surviving manuscripts has shown that none of them, or of their immediate parents, was written by St. Patrick's hand or directly copied from his autograph. We may assume that we owe the continued existence of these two ancient epistles to the originals having been circular letters with several copies contemporaneous with the saint.

The main purpose of this translation is to allow more people to meet and better appreciate the great Apostle to the Irish. Should the explanatory material and notes detract from this goal, the reader must ignore them in favor of a direct encounter with the saint's own words. If you read nothing else between the covers of this book, read Patrick! For the man born Calpurnius Succetus is among the greatest human beings ever to have walked this earth; one who has much to teach us and he speaks more eloquently on his own behalf than anyone else could hope to do.

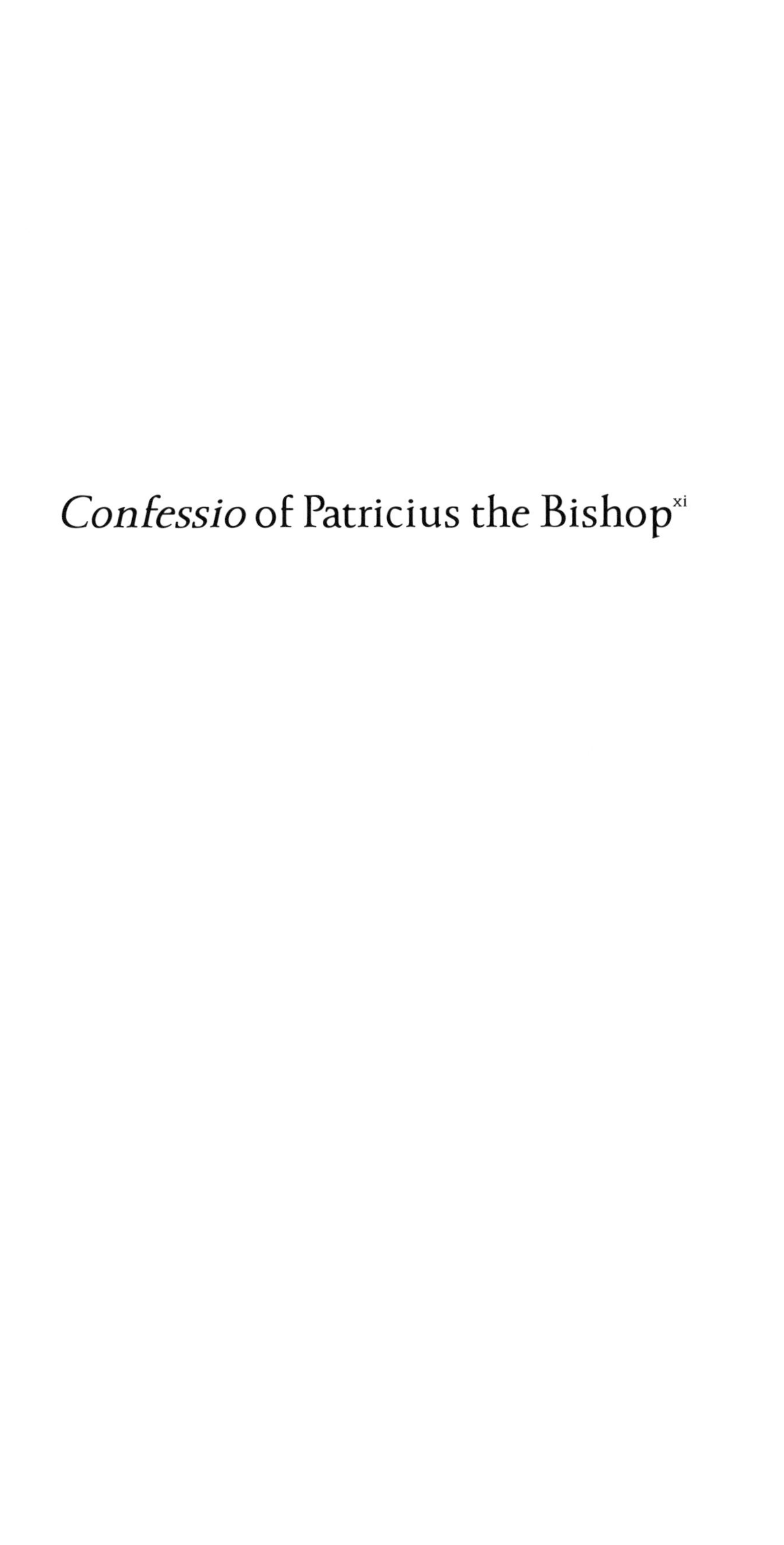

Confessio of Patricius the Bishop[xi]

Genesis

I Patricius, a sinner, most unpolished, least of all the faithful and exceedingly contemptible in the estimation of a great many, had as father Calpurnius, a deacon,[21] son of Potitus, a priest who was from the vicus[22] Bonaven Taberniae.[xii] Nearby he had an estate, "Enon,"[xiii] where I was taken captive. I was then about sixteen years old.

Because I was ignoring the true God, I was led to Ireland in captivity with countless others as we deserved. For we withdrew from God and did not observe His precepts; neither were we obedient to our bishops,[xiv] who kept reminding us of our salvation. "The Lord poured out a windstorm of His living Spirit[xv] upon us, scattering us among many heathens" "even to the ends of the earth," where now my inconsequence[xvi] is to be seen dwelling among foreigners.

There [*in Ireland*] the Lord opened my eyes to my lack of faith so that I would call to mind my failings and turn my whole heart to the Lord my God, who reflected on my weakness and, having pity on my youth and ignorance, took care of me before I had knowledge of Him. Before I was wise, or had distinguished between good and evil, He protected me, consoling me as a father does a son.

This is why I cannot be silent about such a great conferring of privileges and such great grace (nor is it advantageous [*to do so*]), which the Lord has deigned to grant me in the land of my captivity.[xvii] For the way we can repay Him after He corrects us, and we come to knowledge of Him, is to exalt and confess His wonders before every nation under heaven:

> Because there is no other God, neither has there been, nor will there ever be, other than God the Unbegotten Father, who Himself had no beginning,[xviii] from whom all things originate, maintaining all things – as we have come to understand. And we bear witness that His Son, Jesus Christ, has truly always existed with the Father

21 "Calpurnius, a deacon" has caused some to wonder how Patrick could have been so impervious to faith as a boy. During the period of his father's and grandfather's lives, Roman law often changed regarding the duties of landowners and was not uniformly observed, particularly in the provinces. Calpurnius, who was also a decurion, or local senator, as we learn in the *Pastoral Epistle*, may have taken advantage of a legal loophole freeing him from some of the onerous obligations attendant on his class by becoming a deacon, possibly one with little or no faith. For, during his lifetime, a decurion not only had to pay heavy taxes himself but to collect them from others, a task even more onerous than the taxes.

22 *Vicus* can mean a village, hamlet, or quarter of a city. Here it refers to the part of Bononia (Boulogne in northern France) where the shops were, the lower part near the harbor. See endnotes for more details.

> before the birth of the world: spiritually with the Father, ineffably begotten before all beginning. Through Him all things have been made, visible and invisible. He was made man, and, having vanquished death, was received into heaven with the Father, who has given Him all power over every kind of being[23] in heaven, on earth, or in the realms below. May every tongue confess that Jesus Christ, in whom we believe, is Lord and God! We await His coming, some time in the future, as Judge of the living and the dead, who will render to each according to his actions.
>
> On us He has poured out His Spirit abundantly, gift and assurance of immortality, who makes the believing and receptive[xix] capable of becoming children of God and co-heirs with Christ, whom we acknowledge and we adore: one God in a Trinity of holiness.[24]

For He Himself said through the prophet, "Call upon Me in the day of your distress; I shall deliver you and you will glorify Me." Again He says, "Moreover, to explain and praise the works of the Lord bestows honor." So, despite the fact that I am imperfect in many respects, I also desire my "brethren and peers" to know my nature that they may be able to perceive the dedication of my life.[xx]

I am well aware of the testimony of my Lord, Who in the psalm states, "You will destroy those who tell lies." And again He says, "A lying mouth murders the soul." The same Lord says in the gospel, "On the day of judgment people will render an account for the idle words they have uttered." Therefore I ought to dread exceedingly, with fear and trembling, the thought of that day when no one will be able to steal away or hide, but all without exception will render an account of even the least sins before the tribunal of the Lord Christ.

23 The Latin here translated as "every kind of being" is *omne nomen. Nomen* has a deeper meaning, not simply "name" but "being" or "classification of being" as, in this case, the word is followed by three classifications: heavenly, earthly, and subterranean. This usage is related to the one in the note below for "Trinity of holiness." *Nomen* also means "family" or "clan name," a classification within a *gens* or people.

24 Although *Trinitate sacri nominis* is literally translated "Trinity of holy name," that does not convey the meaning. *Trinity of holy being or holiness*, while still imperfectly translating the Latin, attempts to get behind apparent definitions to what is really being said. For *nomen* not only means "name," but also "clan" or the stock from which one descends. In this case, because we are dealing with the Divine "nature," we are speaking of what the Trinity *is*, something beyond our grasp, but certainly holy. One awkward human way of putting it is to say that the family name of the Trinity is "holiness." Another is: holiness is the Trinity's being. Saint John the Theologian says "God is love" so that we may understand that true holiness is love and that we must learn love from the One whose very being defines it.

Apologia

What was the reason I thought about writing for a long time but hesitated until now?[xxi] I feared being cut to pieces by the slander of men because I did not study the way others did who absorbed to the full both law and Sacred Scripture alike and who, from childhood, have never changed their language, but rather perfected the one they had.[25]

But our words and manner of speaking have been translated into a foreign tongue.[26] Indeed it is easy to demonstrate, from the flavor of my writing, the process by which my language was shaped and refined,[xxii] for it is said, "A wise man is discerned by his language: his expressed thought, his skill, as well as what he has learned of truth."

How does an excuse advance the truth, particularly when it anticipates objections? To what extent do I seek in my old age to accomplish what I did not achieve in youth, since my sins prevented my mastering what I studied then?[xxiii] And who will believe me, even if I reiterate what I said before: as a youth, or rather as an almost inarticulate boy, I was captured before I knew what to seek or what to shun?

This is why I blush for shame today and greatly fear to expose my unskillfulness: because I cannot express myself in writing to the concisely eloquent as my spirit and mind desire and my heart's feelings incline. But, although I truly wish I were as gifted as others, I will not keep silent just to avoid criticism.[xxiv] And if it should seem that I put myself forward somewhat in this (with my lack of knowledge and my rather slow tongue), even so it is written: "Stammering tongues will swiftly learn to speak peace."

How much more ought we to aspire, we who are, as Scripture says: "an epistle of Christ for salvation, even unto the ends of the earth"? And, if not eloquent, yet approved and fearless, "inscribed on your hearts, not with ink, but with the Spirit of the living God."

25 *Conf.* (9) Patrick refers to the courses of legal and theological studies pursued by other clerics of his class in Rome and to the difficulty of writing polished Latin when he has been speaking Irish for decades.

26 *Linguam lienam:* Searches for an adjective, *lienam*, only yielded *alienus*, which must be the word Patrick wrote. *Lien, lienis*, a noun meaning "spleen" is obviously irrelevant here. The *foreign tongue* is Irish, the language he had been speaking for nearly three decades and in which he composed his sermons and communications to the Irish converts. His two surviving epistles were in Latin because addressed to his fellow clerics and, in the case of the *Pastoral Epistle*, to a mature flock who understood the language. Coroticus and his men probably understood it as well. Latin would be the only language common to most of his audience.

Again, the Spirit declares: "Even rural life is created by the Most High." As an illustration I, a former rustic and one exiled from his patria (that is to say, not a man of letters),[27] cannot foresee tomorrow. But I do know for certain that before I was humbled I was like a stone lying in deep mud, and yet He-Who-is-Mighty came and, in His compassion, pulled me out.

Even more than that, He actually has elevated me and placed me at the top of the house[28] where I must boldly proclaim my gratitude to the Lord for His great blessings, both here and in eternity – which the human mind is incapable of comprehending.

Marvel, then, all you great and lowly who fear God, and you clever masters of rhetoric![xxv] Listen, therefore, and consider who has raised up foolish me from the midst of those who appear to be wise and learned in law, powerful in discourse and all affairs. He has even inspired me beyond others of this abominable world to be one who, with awe and reverence and without complaint, should faithfully go to that pagan people onto whom Christ's love engrafted me. And He has granted that, if in my life I proved worthy, I might finally truly serve them with humility.

Consequently, from the perspective of faith in the Trinity, it behooves me, without attempting to hold back, to finish making known the "gift of God" and "everlasting liberation";[29] to spread the name of God everywhere, courageously and faithfully so as, even after death, to leave a legacy to the brethren, as well as to my children, countless numbers of whom I have baptised in the Lord.

I was neither worthy nor so distinguished that the Lord should grant this [*elevation*] to his humble servant[xxvi] – after labors and such burdens, after imprisonment, after many years among that pagan people – that He should freely bestow such a great blessing on me for which I neither hoped in my youth nor thought about at any time.

27 *Indoctus*, here translated as "not a man of letters," is more commonly rendered "untaught." Because Patrick was certainly taught, this did not seem the best translation. *Doctus* means "learned, skilled, well-versed, a man of letters, a connoisseur, cunning"; thus *indoctus* may be the opposite of any one of these. Use of this word suggests Patrick's awareness of the views of his audience (that he operates outside the realm of cultivated Roman society and letters and thus is *indoctus*) – and his amusement, since the epistle itself invalidates their criticisms and because their opinions are rendered irrelevant by the emperor's naming him Patricius.

28 *The top of the house* may be an idiom or simply Patrick's way of expressing his elevation to Patricius, the highest Roman rank "in the house," i.e. the Church, to which a cleric could be raised, the only higher imperial positions being those of consul and emperor.

29 The gift of God, *donum dei*, is the Holy Spirit and *consolatio*, "liberation" in Late Latin, is the result of that gift.

Exodus

After I had come to Ireland,[30] therefore, I was daily herding cattle[31] and praying often throughout the day. More and more, the love and fear of God increased in me. Faith was being generated, and the Spirit set in motion, so that in a single day I was praying up to a hundred times, and nearly as much at night. Even while I remained in the woods and on the mountain, I was roused up to prayer before dawn in snow, frost, and rain. Neither did I feel ill nor was there any sloth in me, although only now do I see that it was because the Spirit was burning in me then.

There, in a dream one night, I heard a Voice speaking to me: "It is a good thing you are fasting.[xxvii] Soon you will go to your homeland." After a short while I heard the Voice a second time,[xxviii] saying: "Behold, your ship is ready." It was not nearby, but perhaps one hundred eighty miles distant.[32] I had never been there, nor did I know a single person in that place. From that moment I hoped to run away and, later, I escaped from the man with whom I had been for six years.

I went with the power of God, who directed my journey successfully, and I feared nothing until I came to the ship.[xxix] The ship had set out from its home port the very day I arrived. I said that I had the wherewithal[33] to sail with them, yet the captain was displeased with this. He responded with indignation: "It is useless for you to attempt in any way to go with us!"

30 *Hibernia* is the Latin word for "Ireland." Patrick does not employ it, but uses instead a word derived from Old Irish: *Iverion/Hiberion*. He uses *Hiberionaci*, from the Irish *Iverionaki*, to refer to the Irish people as a whole and *Scotti* for the Irish ruling class. For more explanation of *Hiberione, Hiberionaci* etc. see welshjournals.llgc.org.uk/browse/viewpage/llgcid:1386666/llgc.id:1426378/getText.

31 *Pecora* is translated "cattle" although others have chosen "sheep" or even "pigs." While *pecus, pecoris* can mean other domestic animals, its first meaning is "cattle." Patrick meant "cattle" because Ireland's fifth-century economy was almost entirely cattle-based (cows were even the basic currency) and because he was precise in choosing his words. He would have used *ovis* if he had meant "sheep," or *porca* if he meant "pigs," as he does later in this same section when dealing with the provision of food for the crew that brought him back to Gaul. See P.W. Joyce, *Social History of Ancient Ireland, Vol. 2* (India: Reink Books, 2018) 277-285. *The Tain Bo Cualinge*, the closest thing to an Irish epic, illustrates the role of cattle in early Irish society: Thomas Kinsella, *The Tain* (Oxford: Oxford University Press, 2002 [1969]).

32 *Ducenta milia passus* (about 180 statute miles) is compatible with the distance from *Sliabh Mis* in *Dal n'Araide*, where Patrick herded cattle, to the major southeastern port from which ships sailed to Gaul: *Inbher De* (Arklow).

33 *Unde* or "wherewithal" could not, after six years of slavery, mean money. Instead, it must have meant that Patrick's family would reimburse the captain when he landed at Bononia. The captain's initial refusal to take him on, reveals the saint's habitual disposition: "On the way [*back to the hut*] I began to pray."

After hearing this, I left them to go to the little hut where I was staying. On the way I began to pray and before I had finished my prayer I heard one of them shouting loudly after me: "Come quickly for the men are calling you!" I returned to them immediately and they began saying to me: "Come. We are receiving you based on your assurances.[34] Make an alliance with us in whatever way you prefer." Indeed on that day, I refused to suck their nipples for fear of God.[35] Nevertheless, I hoped to bring some of them to faith in Jesus Christ as they were heathens. We set sail immediately and I maintained this intention in relation to them.

After three days we reached land, and for twenty-eight days we traveled through deserted country.[36] They ran out of food and hunger overcame them. The following day the captain said to me: "What's this, Christian? You say your God is great and all-powerful. Why then can you not pray for us since we are in danger of starving? It is unlikely that we will ever see another human being again."

I spoke to them boldly: "Turn in faith 'with your whole heart to the Lord my God, because to Him nothing is impossible.' Indeed, today He might send you food for your journey until you are filled, because He has abundance everywhere.

And with God's help it happened. Behold, before our very eyes, a herd of pigs appeared on the road. They killed many of them, remaining there two nights well fed, having eaten their fill of meat.[xxx] (Many [*crew members*] had fainted away and been left behind, half-dead, on the road.) After this they gave the greatest thanks to God and I became honorable in their eyes. From that day they had abundant food, even finding some forest honey. They offered me some, but one of them said, "It has been sacrificed." Thank God, I tasted none of it.

34 The "assurances" must be the promise of reimbursement by his relatives on his being returned to Bononia. Because Bononia was so far out of the captain's way, that inconvenience must have motivated his initial reluctance to take Patrick on as a crew member.

35 This refers to a pagan Irish rite of submission which, despite his need to take ship for Gaul, Patrick refuses to perform. See J.F.T. Kelly, "The Escape of Saint Patrick from Ireland" in *Studia Patristica XVIII* (Leuven: Peeters Publishers, 1983) 41-45.

36 Both the length of the sail and the time spent in deserted country confirm that the ship's destination was Gaul, not Britain and thus, that Gaul was Patrick's patria. One day would have been sufficient for a journey to Britain and its western coasts were heavily populated; while much of northwestern Gaul was not, in part due to devastation wrought by marauding barbarians, which explains why the pirates did not encounter anyone for weeks.

That same night, while I was sleeping, Satan tempted me severely in a manner that I shall remember so long as I am in this body. He fell upon me like a huge rock and my limbs were powerless.[37] What inspired me, spiritually inexperienced, to invoke Elias? For, in the midst of these cries, I saw the sun rise into the heavens and, while I was shouting "Elias! Elias!"[xxxi] with all my strength, lo, the brightness of the sun fell down over me, immediately dispersing all my oppression.

I believe that Christ my Lord came to my rescue, and that it was His Spirit crying out on my behalf, and I hope it will be so "on the day of my deep sleep," as He says in the gospel. "On that day" the Lord declares, "it will not be you who speak, but the Spirit of your Father who speaks in you."

For once again, after all those years [*as a slave*], I was, from the very first night I stayed with them, still a captive. But then I heard the Divine Voice saying to me: "You will be with them for two months," which was what happened. On the sixtieth night the Lord released me from them.

He continued to provide food, fire, and dry weather every day for us until we reached human beings on the tenth day. As I mentioned above, we traveled through the wilderness for twenty-eight days and, on the night when we arrived among humans, really had no food left.

After a few years in the Britains,[38][xxxii] I was once again with my relatives[39] who received me as the son,[xxxiii] and out of trustworthiness requested that I should never depart from them, after having undergone such great sufferings. And it was there that I saw in a dream the man named Victoricus[40] coming, as though from Ireland, with innumerable letters.[xxxiv] He gave me one and I read the beginning of a letter containing "The Call of the Irish."

37 The oppression Patrick sees as severe demonic temptation was the result of his belated discovery that he had been enslaved again "from the very first night I stayed with them" – and that the ship was not headed for Bononia at all. The captain's change of heart regarding Patrick's membership in the crew must have been a calculation that this strapping young man would be a great addition to his workforce, one he need not pay or actually deliver to his family, i.e. a slave.

38 Patrick has just mentioned spending two months with his captors. Now he alludes to *a few years in the Britains* so we understand that he does not return to Bononia until he is twenty-four or twenty-five, since he was about twenty-two at the end of his six years as a slave in Ireland.

39 *Parens, parentis* may mean parent, ancestor, or relative. The epistles indicate that Patrick's father had predeceased him, and here reveal that he was acknowledged as "the son," his father's heir, confirmed by his inheriting the family property. Thus "relative" is the meaning in this context.

40 Saint Victoricus, patron saint and first bishop of Bononia, with St. Fuscianus, brought the Christian faith to Bononia and founded its first church at the end of the third century. That church, the only church at Boulogne remembered by chroniclers for the first six Christian centuries, is the one Potitus served, the one near his estate on the Liane.

While I was reading the first part of it aloud, at the same moment I imagined hearing the summons[41] of those very people who lived by the forest of the Ulaid near the Western Sea. They cried out, as if with one mouth: "We beg you, chaste young man,[xxxv] to come and help us."[xxxvi] It pierced my heart so that I could read no further. Such I experienced because, thanks be to God, after many years the Lord made it happen according to their loud supplications.

On a different night, ("I know not, God knows" whether within or beside me), I listened to the most erudite words without comprehending them until, when the oration ended, One spoke out thus: "He Who has laid down His life for you is the One speaking within you." On that account, I woke up rejoicing.

Another time I perceived Him praying inside me as though I were within my body, but heard Him above me, that is, above the interior person. There He was praying strenuously with sighs. In the middle of all this I was stupefied, wondering and pondering who was praying in me. At the end of the prayer, He revealed that He was the Spirit.[42]

41 *Vox*, meaning "voice," "calling out" or "call" is, in this instance, translated "summons" because of the context and because he speaks of multiple people without making vox plural: "voices." It also means "call by name," personalizing the summons. This call has a clearly defined, personal object.

42 Patrick borrows phraseology from St. Paul in 2 Cor.12 to describe an experience of mystical prayer that occurred after the dream in which Victoricus approached him with the letters from Ireland. He identifies with Paul, his own scriptural quotations being heavily weighted in favor of those from the Apostle to the Gentiles, for he sees himself also bringing the Good News to "gentiles."

Leviticus

In this way I have learned by experience, taking to heart what the Apostle[43] says: "The Spirit aids the infirmities of our prayer because we know not for what we ought to pray, but the Spirit Himself pleads inexpressible things for us with indescribable sighs." Again and again, the Lord our Advocate petitions for us.[xxxvii]

When tried by some of my elders, who came into court against me and presented my sins in opposition to my arduous episcopacy,[44] undoubtedly, on that day, I sustained a great blow – as though I should perish here and in eternity. Yet the Lord spared a convert, alien for the sake of His own gracious being,[xxxviii] powerfully coming to my support in this humiliation – since I did not fall into shame and dishonor erroneously. I pray God that it not be reckoned to them as sin.

Thirty years after the fact, they discovered a plausible pretext to[45] *discredit me: a mere word I had confessed before I was a deacon. Anxious and in a melancholy state of mind, I disclosed to my closest friend what I had done in my boyhood, more accurately, in one hour, for I had not yet acquired self-mastery. "I do not know, God knows," if I was even fifteen years old.*

I did not believe in the living God, nor had I from my baptism,[xxxix] *but remained in death and unbelief until I was severely chastised; in truth, humiliated by daily hunger and nakedness. Instead, in Ireland I was persevering involuntarily*[46] *until the time I nearly perished. But this was actually a blessing since, because of it, I have been corrected by the Lord.*

He has shaped me so that today I might be what was for so long beyond my capability. Now I have the care of, or rather am fully occupied with, the salvation of others – when once I did not even consider my own.

43 Saint Paul, in Rom. 8:26.

44 The saint alludes more specifically to the elders' reservations in **Numbers:** *Conf.* (46).

45 This section, in italics for clarification, is a long aside in which Patrick explains the source of the accusations presented at his episcopal hearing and resurrected decades later after his elevation to Patricius.

46 *Contra Hiberione non sponte pergebam:* Patrick contrasts his unwilling slavery as an unbeliever in Ireland with his transformation by God's grace: faithful acceptance of his situation becoming a blessing for himself and others.

As I was saying, on the night of the day I was censured by those previously mentioned, I saw in a dream[xl] the written accusation dishonoring my character. At the same time I heard the Divine Voice saying to me: "We have viewed with disapproval the honor of the bishop-elect's[47] character stripped bare." He did not say, "*You* have viewed, with disapproval," but rather "*We* have viewed with disapproval," as though He had united Himself to me, just as He has said, "He who attacks you attacks the apple of my eye." [xli]

This is why I am thankful to Him Who has strengthened me in everything, hindering neither the departure on which I had resolved, nor the task received from Christ my Lord. Rather, I sensed within myself no little power coming from Him and my faith was manifest before God and men. Therefore, I confidently state that my conscience neither reproaches me now nor for the future. God is my witness that I have not lied in what I have recounted to you.

Yet I grieve rather for my dearest friend. Why did we deserve to hear such testimony from him to whom I had entrusted my very soul?[xlii] Nevertheless, I gained information from certain of the brethren before that hearing, for I was not present, neither was I in the Britains,[48] nor was it my idea that he was going to accuse me – in my absence![xliii]

He is the person who had told me with his own mouth: **"See, you are to be raised to the episcopate of which I was unworthy."**[49] But why did it occur to him afterward, in the sight of everyone, good and bad, to dishonor me publicly over something he had freely chosen not to censure, as did the Lord, Who is greater than all?

47 The noun *designatus* has been changed by translators into a verb, "to designate" or to a proper name, "Designatus," assigned to Patrick's treacherous friend. But Roman law practice of the period establishes its actual definition, making it clear that the word applies to Patrick, not to his "friend."

One chosen for high secular or ecclesiastical Roman office was *designatus* until after a hearing examining his character, abilities, and credentials. Only after passing successfully through this examination did he assume office. "Bishop-elect" is the closest English term for *designatus* in this context.

This was not a trial, but the regulation fifth-century pre-ordination hearing, and thus it occurred in Gaul before the saint left for Ireland as bishop. See William Smith, *A Dictionary of Christian Antiquities, Vol. I* (London: John Murray, 1875) p. 1481 for more about such hearings. Admission to orders required a candidate to be freeborn, of good character, of a certain age, unconvicted of crime, and possessed of sufficient property to discharge the duties of his office.

48 Patrick was in Boulogne, not at his hearing, about which he was informed by his brethren who must have travelled from Auxerre where it was held, (or sent a messenger) to Boulogne, where he was serving. Obviously, though, he was able to return in time to testify on his own behalf before the conclusion of the hearing since he was acquitted, and ordained without *hindering . . . the departure on which I had resolved.*

49 The sentence is in boldface because, in chiastic construction, a work's central sentence is the most significant. In this instance it exposes the motive of Patrick's duplicitous friend: envy. The friend understood himself to be unworthy of the episcopacy to which Patrick was being elevated; less worthy than Patrick who never went to Rome, who came late to his rhetorical studies because of his years of slavery in Ireland. The same sin, envy, is found at the center of the *Pastoral Epistle* as the cause of that betrayal as well.

Enough said. I must not lose sight of the gift of God lavished on us "in the land of my captivity" because it was at that time that I energetically sought Him and found Him. It is my belief that He kept me from all misfortunes "through His indwelling Spirit" who has been unceasingly active in me until this day. Another bold remark! Yet God knows that, if the [*merely*] human in me had expressed itself, perhaps I would have held my tongue for the sake of Christ's love.[50]

This is why I give ceaseless thanks to my God Who kept me faithful on the day of my testing so that now I might confidently offer Him my soul as a living sacrifice to Christ, my Lord who has preserved me from all my perils so that I too might ask: "Who am I, Lord?" or "What is my calling?" You have revealed Yourself to me with so much divine inspiration that today, among pagans, I might constantly "exalt and acknowledge the magnitude of Your being"[xliv] wherever I am, not only when things go well but also under pressure."

Thus, whatever happens to me, good or evil, I ought to bear equally, always giving thanks to God who has shown me that I should rely on Him completely. He heard me so that, in the last days, I, unskilled, might dare to undertake this holy and wondrous work in order that, to some extent, I should follow in the footsteps of those who long ago the Lord foretold would be heralds of His gospel "for a witness to all peoples before the end of the world."

As to this, we have observed it [*to be*] so. Accordingly it has been fulfilled: behold, we are witnesses that the gospel has been proclaimed to the place beyond which there is no one.

50 The saint kept silent about this episode until the end of his life when it became clear that exposing the truth of it was necessary to a greater Christian love than that for one individual, his duplicitous friend, whose reputation he had shielded for so many years by his silence. The future success of the Irish mission depended in part on his converts' trust in Patrick's character. But elevation to Patricius had stirred up old rumors from his episcopal hearing which, without rebuttal, could cast doubt on the founder of the Irish missions. Without bitterness or anger, Patrick dissipates these rumors simply and passes on immediately to praise and thanks for "the gift of God (*donum Dei*, the Holy Spirit) lavished on us."

Numbers

It is too tedious to explain my work in whole or in part. [*Instead*] I shall briefly relate how God Most Holy often liberated me from slavery and twelve perils[51] threatening my life, as well as from many snares and things I am unable to express in words.[xlv] I do not wish to bore my readers, but God, who knows all before it happens, is my authority that I, an insignificant orphan,[xlvi] an unenlightened man, was frequently advised by His divine counsel.

Whence came this wisdom? It was not in me, who neither knew the number of his days nor had discernment of God. From what source was the subsequent gift, so great, so salutary, to know and to love God so dearly that I would relinquish homeland and near relations?

Many presents were offered to me with weeping and tears, but I offended the donors and also, without intending to, certain of my elders. Yet, with God guiding, I neither conceded nor acquiesced to them in any way, thanks, not to me but to God who conquers in me, and I firmly withstood them all.

In what way had I come to preach the gospel to Irish heathens? [*I had come*] to suffer outrages from unbelievers "that I might hear taunts about my living abroad," and [*to endure*] many persecutions "even to the extent of imprisonment" that I might surrender my freeborn status[52] for the advantage of others, and if found worthy, I quickly add, [*to surrender*] even my life freely and without delay for His sake.[xlvii] There [*in Ireland*] I choose to spend my life until death, if the Lord allows me, for I am very much in debt to God, who gave me sufficient grace so that through me many people should be reborn in Him, and afterwards brought to maturity.

Everywhere clergy should be ordained for them [*the Irish*], a congregation[xlviii] recently coming to belief, which the Lord has purchased from the farthest corners of the earth, since in times past He predicted through His prophets: "Pagans will come to you from the ends of the earth and they will say: 'The idols our fathers fashioned were false and there is no advantage to them.'"

51 No attempt has been made here to identify the twelve perils because we only have the witness of these two epistles and Patrick may be alluding to events not included in them.

52 Patrick's reasons for undertaking the Irish mission (not the riches his enemies suspected as his motivation for it) mention surrendering his "freeborn status." He refers to the same thing in Epist. (10) where he states that he sold his "noble status." Patrick's status as a Roman noble was linked to property and to responsibility for serving in the local *curia*. He sold his inherited property in order to have the money to conduct his Irish mission. There being no central source of money for the support of churches, bishops were expected to supply such support themselves, one reason why they were almost always of the nobility.

The saint contrasts his refusal of riches legitimately offered to him with the "riches" he actually received: insults, persecutions, imprisonment and the surrender of his property for the mission.

And again: "I have placed you as a light among gentiles so that you may exist for the purpose of salvation as far as the ends of the earth." There [*at the ends of the earth, in Ireland*] I choose to await the fulfillment of His promise, who certainly never deceives, just as it was promised in the Gospel: "They will come from the East and the West and they will recline at table with Abraham, Isaac and Jacob."

Thus we have confidence that believers will come from all over the world. On that account, it is necessary to fish well and with loving care, as the Lord advises and teaches, saying: "Come, follow me and I shall make you fishers of men." Again He says through the prophets: "Behold I send forth fishermen and many hunters," and so forth.

That is why it is especially fitting to spread our nets so that a multitude, abundant and diverse, should be acquired for God, and everywhere there should be clergy to baptise and exhort a needy people longing for what they lack. For the Lord in the gospel reminds [*us*] and teaches, saying: "Go now, therefore, and instruct all nations, baptising them in the name of the Father and of the Son and of the Holy Spirit, teaching them to observe all that I have commanded you" and, "Behold, I shall be with you all days until the consummation of the age."

Another time He says, "Go therefore into the whole world; preach the gospel to every creature. He who believes and is baptised will be saved. He who does not believe will be condemned." And again: "Proclaim this good news of the Kingdom to the whole world for a witness to all heathens – and then the end will come."

In the same manner, the Lord fortells through the prophet, saying: "And in the last days, I shall generously pour out my Spirit over all flesh and your sons and daughters will prophesy; your youths will see visions and your old men will dream dreams. Indeed I shall pour out my Spirit upon my servants and handmaidens and they will prophesy." "In Hosea He says, 'Those who were not my people I shall call "my people," and those who have not obtained mercy, "they who have obtained mercy." And in that place where once He said "You are not my People," there they shall be called children of the living God.'"

Moreover in Ireland, those who had no conception of God, until now worshiping only idols and impure things, have recently been made a Christian congregation of the Lord and are called children of God. Sons of the *Scotti*[xlix] and daughters of kings are regarded as monks and virgins of Christ.[53]

53 The placement of *Sons of the Scotti and daughters of kings* at the chiastic center of **Numbers**, his defense of himself and his mission, indicates that Patrick considers the dedication of so many to religious life to be the crowning achievement of his ministry and "proof of the pudding."

There was even one blessed woman of the *Scotti*, nobly born, and most beautiful as a mature woman, whom I baptised. After a few days she came to us for one motive, confiding to us that she had received advice from an envoy[54] of God, counseling her to dedicate her virginity to Christ and that she should draw near to God. Thanks be to God, on the sixth day after this wonderful one, she most eagerly espoused that [*life*], because all virgins of God act in this manner, even without their fathers' consent, suffering persecutions and false accusations from their own relatives.

Nevertheless, their number increases. We do not know the number of those born of our "begetting" apart from widows and chaste women. Among them slave-girls have most to suffer, even enduring terrors and threats. But the Lord has given grace to many of his handmaidens because, despite being forbidden, they still bravely persevere.

Furthermore, even had I wished to leave them [*the Irish converts*] in order to proceed to the Britains, and most gladly made preparations to go as if to homeland and relatives,[55] nay, even all the way to the Gauls[l] to visit the brethren[56] that I might see the faces of my Lord's saints (God knows what I especially preferred!), I was bound by the Spirit, Who declared to me that, if I should do this I should be answerable in the future. I am afraid of destroying the difficult work that I have begun.

Not I, but Christ the Lord, has commanded that I should come to be with them [*the Irish*] for the rest of my life, God willing, and He will protect me from every evil path so that I do not sin before Him. I trust this is what I ought to do, yet my faith is not in myself. For, so long as I am in this mortal body, he [*Satan*] who daily strives to turn me from the faith and integrity of true religion is vigorous to the end of my life in Christ my Lord. The unruly flesh is always drawn toward death, that is, toward illicit allurements.

54 *Nuntio* is often translated "angel" transforming this into a supernatural event. In Late Latin *nuntio* means someone who preaches the Good News, in this case, probably a cleric who advised the young woman.

55 There was almost certainly no immediate family left to visit and no home (he had sold his property). *Quasi ad patriam et parentes*, meaning *almost, nearly* or *as if* to homeland and relatives suggests that Patrick would love to go back to Bononia, but that it was not quite his homeland any more, nor, perhaps, any living there quite his relatives.

56 The saint gives his reason (his vow) for never leaving Ireland, never returning to visit relatives and brethren in Gaul. In so doing he distinguishes the place where his family resides from "the Gauls," where his brethren are. Auxerre was in "the Gauls" proper: *Lugdunensis*; thus, since his family lived in *Belgica II*, his home was not *all the way to the Gauls*. His use of *parens* to mean "relatives" is underscored here when, writing at the end of his long life, he could not be contemplating visiting parents, especially since his father had died when he was young and his failure ever to mention his mother may mean that she too died early.

I understand, to some extent, why I have not lived a perfect life like other believers.[57] But I confess to my Lord without blushing in His sight, because I do not lie: from the time I knew Him in my youth the love and fear of God has grown in me and, by God's grace, I have kept the faith until now. Let him who wishes laugh and insult. I shall not be silent, nor shall I conceal signs and wonders shown to me by the Lord many years before they came to pass, for He knows everything, even before time's division into ages.

This is why I ought to give unceasing thanks to God, who has often been indulgent toward my lack of wisdom, my negligence. On more than one occasion He would not become angry with me who, though given support, did not promptly accept the task I was shown, or follow at the suggestion of the Spirit. The Lord had compassion on me countless times because He saw that I was prepared, but did not know what to do under the circumstances.

For many were against this undertaking.[58] They even spoke against me behind my back saying, "Why does this man send himself into danger among hostile people who know not God?"[li] This was not from malice; it just did not seem wise to them, as I myself bear witness, on account of my lack of polish.[59] I was slow to recognize the grace that was in me then. Now I comprehend what I ought to have understood earlier.[lii]

Accordingly, at this very time, I have frankly explained to my brethren and fellow servants who have believed in me because of what I have proclaimed and still do proclaim in order to fortify and establish your faith.[60] If only you will try harder and do more powerful deeds this will be my glory for "a wise son is the glory of his father."

You know, as does God, how I have lived among you from my youth[61] in plain-spoken faith and sincerity of heart. Even to the heathens among whom I dwell, I have kept, and shall keep, my word. God knows I have deceived

57 This appears to refer to the agnosticism of his boyhood.

58 These elders are the ones referred to in **Leviticus** who questioned Patrick's fitness for the Irish mission, in part because the great Palladius' mission had failed after less than a year in Hibernia among those already Christian, not among the more challenging Ulster pagans Patrick hoped to convert.

59 "lack of polish," i.e. *rusticitas*.

60 The saint here acknowledges that, in addition to his *brethren and peers (cognati)* in Gaul, his fellow clerics in Ireland are among his addressees, and that explanations are needed *in order to fortify and establish your faith*. Unless baseless rumors or distortions are countered, Patrick foresees the possibility that the faith of those who must carry on the work he has begun may be shaken.

61 Roman youth, *juventus*, spanned the years between twenty and forty-five. The statement Patrick makes about living among them from his youth holds true primarily for his brethren and cognati in Gaul: his fellow deacons and bishops, but it was also true for Gallic clerics in Ireland who had known him before he arrived in Ireland as bishop, as well as the Irish who knew him as a slave.

none of them. Neither do I think of so doing, on God's account and that of His Church, lest I stir up persecution against it and all of us and lest the name of the Lord be blasphemed through me. For it is written: "Woe to the man through whom the name of the Lord is blasphemed."

Although I am "naive in all things," nevertheless in some respects I have striven to be on my guard even from Christian brethren, virgins of Christ, and religious women who were volunteering small gifts. They cast their ornaments on the altar and I kept returning them.

They were offended by me; why was I doing this? I did it for the hope of what endures. Thus I scrupulously preserved myself that they might ensnare neither me, nor the servants of my household, in any legal charge of infidelity. I did not give unbelievers the slightest opportunity to slander or speak ill.

Was I expecting, perhaps, even half a scruple[62] from any of the thousands I baptised? Prove it to me and I will pay you back.[63] Or if, when the Lord ordained clerics everywhere through my humble person and I performed the service for free, I asked any of them for even the price of my shoe, tell me to my face and I will pay you back more. I have spent for you so that they [*the thousands of potential converts*] might receive me.

Among you, and everywhere, I have traveled for your sake into many perils, even to the remotest places beyond which no one lived and where no one had ever come to baptise, to ordain clergy, or to perfect people in their faith. By the Lord's grace, I have done all this for your eternal welfare, lovingly and willingly.

Occasionally I gave presents to the kings in addition to the fee I paid their sons[liii] who travel along with me. Nevertheless they arrested me with my companions and on that day were most eager to kill me. But the time had not yet come. They seized everything they found with us and constrained me with chains. On the fourteenth day, the Lord delivered me from their power. Our belongings were given back to us, with the help of God and indispensable friends we had previously met.

62 A scruple was the smallest part of any measure. See A.R. Burns, *Money and Monetary Policy* (Oxford/New York: 1996).

63 In this section Patrick more particularly addresses the Irish clergy and converts, doing so in such a way as to make one wonder whether the revived Gallo-Roman rumors about Patrick's motives in undertaking the mission had begun to influence some in Ireland to also raise questions. His use of "you" in this section is clearly directed at all those with and for whom he had labored in Ireland.

Furthermore, you have witnessed how much I paid out to brehons in all the territories[64] I visited frequently. I calculate that I gave them no less than the value of fifteen men so that you might delight in me, as I will always enjoy you in God. I have no regrets, nor is it enough that I still spend and shall spend even more. The Lord has the power to grant that soon I shall be [*entirely*] spent for your souls.

64 *Brehons* is how I have translated *qui judicabant*: those who judged. *Brehon* is the Irish word for judge and describes the functions of a judge in Irish society better than the English word. *Brehons* were of the druidic caste, highly respected and powerful, especially *Ollamh Brehons* who advised the kings. Their permission was required for travel in territories over which they held sway and a fee accompanied the granting of such permissions. At formal gatherings not even the king could speak before his *brehon*.

Deuteronomy

Behold, I call God as witness that I do not lie concerning my life.[65] I have written to you neither as an occasion for flattery, nor out of avarice or hope of preferment[66] from any of you. For honor, as yet invisible but believed in the heart,[liv] suffices. Furthermore, He who promised salvation is faithful and never lies.

Even now in this present age I see myself exalted beyond measure by the Lord.[67] I was neither worthy nor so remarkable that He should distinguish me, while I most certainly know that poverty and adversity have suited me better than riches and luxury. Besides, Christ the Lord also was poor on our account. Even had I wished for them [*riches and luxury*], I have, at this time, no resources, being very ill and unproductive.[68]

Not that I condemn myself because every day I expect either a massacre, or that I will be defrauded, returned to slavery, or some such calamity. For, on account of the heavenly promises, I fear none of these things since I have cast myself into the hand of almighty God Who is supreme everywhere.

As the prophet says: "Submit your will to God and He will take care of you." Behold, now I commit my life to my most faithful God Whose ambassador I am in my obscurity. Indeed, because He "is no respecter of persons," He chose me for this duty to be one from among His least.

65 At about the same distance from the end of the *Confessio* as his first words about lying are from the beginning, Patrick once more calls on God to witness that he does not lie about his life. He also does this in the center of the epistle just before he reveals that his best friend betrayed him at his hearing.

66 This is an instance of the saint's tongue-in-cheek humor. His audience is unlikely to flatter him after the *un*flattering implications much of the epistle directs at some of his *brethren and peers*. Furthermore, if avarice had not motivated the saint during the previous decades of his mission, it is absurd to think that the riches of the world would suddenly appeal now, when he was about to go where he could have no use for them.

He has already been elevated to *the top of the house* so there can be no *hope of preferment* resulting from this epistle. He could not even become a metropolitan bishop since no metropolis existed in Ireland at the time and, even if it had, the saint had reached a stage in his life when he would be physically unable to execute the office.

67 Another reference to elevation to Patrician status, reminding us that this honor *as yet invisible, but believed in the heart,* is the catalyst for the epistle. The allusion to *riches and luxury* must refer either to what he had sacrificed in order to serve in Ireland or to the fact that material rewards either did not accompany the office of Patricius, or had not arrived.

68 The saint allows us to see the state of his health and finances at the end of his life, as well as his precarious position vis a vis some of the pagans who oppose what he is doing. His state of soul remains so completely eucharistic, so full of thanksgiving for his many blessings, that he asks what more he can do. The only thing left is martyrdom, which he is perfectly willing, more accurately, eager, to undergo.

What shall I return to Him for all He has given to me? What shall I say or promise my Lord, when I can do nothing unless He enables me? He searches the depths of a person until He is satisfied and I was ready and eager to be allowed to drink from His chalice, just as He has permitted others who have loved Him.

On that account, [*the fact that, for love of God, Patrick was ready "to drink from His chalice"*] may God never allow me to let His own people slip away[lv] whom He has gathered from the ends of the earth. I pray that He will give me perseverance and grant that I may be a faithful witness to Him until death, for the sake of my God.

If I have ever accomplished anything good on behalf of my God Whom I love dearly, I beg Him to allow me to shed my blood with those disciples and captives for the sake of His holiness, even should I lie unburied, or my corpse be torn most violently limb from limb by dogs or eaten by wild beasts or the birds of the air. If this happens to me, I judge with certitude that I will have gained life through my body.[69]

> For without doubt on that day we shall rise again in the brightness of the Sun:[70] that is, in the glory of Jesus Christ our Redeemer. As children of the living God, and co-heirs with Christ, we shall be shaped in His image, since from Him, through Him, and in Him we are to reign.
>
> But the sun that we see, raised for us by His daily command, will never reign nor will its brilliance endure. Unfortunately, all who worship it will descend unhappily, wretchedly, to chastisement.
>
> We, however, believe in and worship the true Sun, Christ, Who is incorruptible, as is one who does His will. Such a one will remain for eternity in the same way Christ remains for eternity, Who reigns with God the Father Almighty and with the Holy Spirit through all ages of ages. Amen.

69 The following hymn-like expression of faith using sun-imagery is completely orthodox, but Patrick's preference for that imagery is almost certainly influenced by pagan Irish sun worship. He had been able to persuade his converts that what they had worshiped was only an icon of the true Sun, Jesus Christ, Who alone could bestow on them the fullness of life for which they instinctively yearned.

70 Lest we confine the errors of sun worship to pagans on the fringes of the known world, at this same period, Pope Leo I rebuked members of his flock, on the steps of St. Peter's, for reverencing the sun. Henry Chadwick, *The Early Church* (New York: Dorset Press, 1967) 126-127. At this point, we see the radiantly poetic heart of this man on the verge of death. His circumstances have little to recommend them, but they are irrelevant. If the epistle offers a likeness of its author, the end of it has become an icon.

Look, allow me to reiterate briefly what I am expressing through the words of my testimony:[71] I bear witness in truth and in joy of heart before God and His holy angels that I have never had reasons other than the Gospel and its promises for going back to that pagan people from whom I barely escaped before.

Therefore I entreat believers and those who fear God, whoever may have thought it worthwhile to read, or rather to accept, this writing that Patricius, a manifestly inept sinner, has written down in Ireland: if I have accomplished or explained any slight thing according to God's will, let no one ever attribute it to my lack of discernment. Then bear witness: it must be believed most truly that it was the "donum Dei."[72] [lvii]

This is my testimony before I die.

71 The Latin word for *witness* or *testimony* is *confessio*. It is employed in Patrick's final sentence as a summing up of the entire epistle. In this context, it could easily be translated "praise," since that is what Patrick's witness is. However, the basic legal sense of the word would be lost and, by choosing *confessio*, Patrick intends to carry out the theme of a courtroom drama. Inextricably linked to his eucharistic praise of God in this letter is the necessary defense he must mount to ensure that praise of God will live on in the Irish people.

72 The saint's final statement emphasizes that his success in Ireland was due to the *donum Dei*, the Holy Spirit, not some *felix culpa*, some happy fault, or accident of his own. Taken as a whole, the epistle is entirely Trinitarian, threaded throughout with allusions to the Holy Spirit. Patrick's experience of the Triune God refined his understanding to an uncommon penetration of the Divine Mystery. What happened in Ireland through his labors was the product of intelligent design: God's. But the sophistication of this epistle should also demonstrate that its author was no clumsy, unconscious tool in God's hands, no ignoramus.

Preface to The Pastoral Epistle

Saint Patrick's *Pastoral Epistle*, commonly known as his *Letter to the Soldiers of Coroticus*, was written close in time to the *Confessio*, after his Irish mission had been well established and after he had been made Patricius, since both epistles begin *Ego Patricius*.

Both letters mention the multitude of individuals inspired to embrace the religious state as well as the saint's age, poverty, and infirmity, all aspects of the final period of his life. And there are thematic similarities in both epistles, as though the saint had, as he neared death, distilled certain experiences and perceptions to adamantine conviction.

I believe that the *Confessio* was written before the *Pastoral Epistle* because the incident provoking the latter was of such a nature that it would have impacted a *Confessio* written subsequent to it. The betrayal (and its cause) described in the *Pastoral Epistle* not only echoes an earlier betrayal at the heart of the *Confessio*, but Patrick seems to perceive and express it through the same cognitive and literary lenses.

Composed for entirely different reasons from those inspiring his *Confessio*, Patrick's *Pastoral Epistle* is the impassioned response of a shepherd to a direct assault on his flock and on the Kingdom of God being established in Ireland.

Newly baptised Irish Christians, holy chrism still shining on their foreheads, had been brutally attacked by Coroticus and his British outlaws with the help of apostates from Patrick's flock. Men were murdered, and women captured to be sold in Britain. Since, as it now appears, the epistle was written toward the very end of the saint's life, the event provoking it acquires more tragic and sinister aspects.

For, horrendous as it was, had the attack occurred earlier, at least there would have been time for the saint to mend the rent in the fabric of his mission. This savage and sacrilegious crime may have functioned as the martyrdom for which the saint prayed at the end of his *Confessio*. Patrick was being tried like Abraham and like Job. And, throughout the epistle, as with them, we see humble, faithful love triumphing.

Addressees

An important difference between the present interpretation of the *Pastoral Epistle* and that of other scholars results from an evolution of understanding that clarified the epistle's intended audience. Neither Coroticus nor his men were likely to find the arguments and pleadings of Patricius the bishop compelling. Apostates, however, familiar with the tenets of Christianity, bound intimately by blood, and previously by faith, to those they had just betrayed were potentially capable of the repentance to which the saint exhorted them.

The proper translation of *socii Scottorum atque Pictorum apostatarumque,* as *associates of Scotti, and even of Picts and apostates*, exposes the primary addressees of this epistle and explains why its title has been changed to reflect that discovery. Others have translated the sentence: *associates of Scotti* (or Irish) *and apostate Picts*. This is incorrect for three reasons.

The first reason is that such translators are ignoring the *que* (the second "and") at the end of *apostatarum*. Patrick is speaking of three groups, not two: *Scotti and even of Picts and apostates*. Otherwise the Latin sentence would read *socii Scottorum atque Pictorum apostatorum*. Patrick uses *atque* rather than *que* for emphasis because *atque* can be translated *and even* and was used to contrast as well as to link. The *que* at the end of *apostatarum* serves to link apostates and Picts more intimately with each other while, at the same time it subtly contrasts them both with the less objectionable Scotti. Also, *que* gives prominence to the word to which it adheres: *apostatarum*.

The second error in the common translation is that *apostata* is a Late Latin noun, not an adjective. Although sometimes used as an adjective, it is not so employed here because of the suffix *que*.[73] Thus the Picts are not being described as apostates, but rather, two groups, despised for different reasons, are being closely connected by association with each other, as demonstrated by the suffix *que*.

A third reason the common translation is incorrect is that the Scottish Picts, with whom most scholars have identified our apostates, could hardly have deserted a faith to which they had yet to be converted. The mistranslation of this line has been used as proof of the early conversion of the Picts by St. Ninian in the late fourth century, a theory otherwise lacking written or archaeological evidence to support it.

For those mistrustful of ancient traditions about St. Ninian and Whithorn as being far too early, given what else is known about the area in 397 when Ninian was supposed to have been converting the Scottish Picts, Thomas Owen Clancy's article "The Real St. Ninian"[74] supplies intellectual relief. Ninian

73 Additionally, if the word were being used as an adjective modifying *Pictorum*, the ending would be masculine: *apostatorum* rather than *apostatarum*. *Apostata* is not only a noun, it is feminine as Patrick knows. To modify *Pictorum* as an adjective, the ending would have to agree in gender.

74 Thomas Owen Clancy, "The Real St. Ninian" in *The Innes Review Vol.52, No.1* (Edinburgh: Edinburgh University Press, 2001) 1-28.

turns out to be a misprint for *Finian* or *Vinniau*, an Irish saint connected with Whithorn who flourished in the sixth century, not the fourth. This is more in accord with historical and archaeological evidence, or the lack thereof.

Although the epistle does mention Coroticus and his confederates and insists that the letter be read to them, Patrick is actually addressing his Christian flock as their bishop, both those who remain in it and have some contact or relation to those who have abandoned their faith to betray their brethren, and the apostates themselves.

While at times the saint specifically exhorts the faithful, and the letter is to *be displayed, recorded and sent to the warriors of Coroticus* and *be read before all the people, even in the presence of Coroticus himself,*[75] his prime targets remain the apostates who, he hopes, will return to the fold, assist in persuading the Britons to release captives and, perhaps, even give back some of the stolen goods. For he cannot hope to reach apostates who have allied themselves with Coroticus unless his words are also made available to the outlaws.

Coroticus' men have shown by the acts they committed and by their response to the first delegation from the Christian community (scornfully laughing at and imprisoning its members, all clerics)[76] that they are hardened criminals. The apostates, on the other hand, may have been seduced by greed to cooperate in an operation that was considerably more evil than simple theft, perhaps more evil than they had bargained for. If so, they may well have had regrets. Patrick obviously hopes that the combination of fear of the eternal consequences of their acts, along with hope of forgiveness and regeneration, will reclaim at least some of their number.

The saint is simply too intelligent and too experienced a missioner to waste words on those impervious to them, or to address an epistle to those he calls *fellow citizens of demons*. The letter is being sent to Coroticus as the leader of the raid, but Patrick's well-designed epistle is not aiming primarily at him or his men since the arguments the saint employs would be poor choices if pagan outlaws were his main targets.

Structure

The fourfold division of the epistle is Dr. David Howlett's "and putatively Patrick's."[77] While, like the *Confessio*, the letter is composed chiastically, it is

75 *Epist.* (2) and (21).

76 *Ibid.* (3).

77 Howlett, *op. cit.* 25.

neither so complex nor so long. Insofar as this is the official communication of a bishop, it is formal, but neither the occasion nor its intended audience warrants the intricate artistic development of themes characteristic of the *Confessio*. Still, the *Pastoral Epistle* does not lack artistry or complexity. Far from it. Its construction just does not rise to the extraordinary level of intricacy exhibited in the *Confessio*.

The *Pastoral Epistle* is a bit like a symphony with recurring motifs that crescendo to a climax intended to move its hearers, particularly the apostates, to realize the consequences of what they have done so they might repent and return to the flock. The saint also hopes his rhetoric will persuade those he addresses to return captives and booty insofar as that is possible. But temporal concerns are totally subordinate to the saint's vision of ultimate reality. Patrick sees all in the light of eternity.

In Part I the saint establishes the source of his authority, God and the Church, describing the criminals as *belonging to the Enemy* in the harshest, most vivid and contemptuous way, before giving an account of their crimes. In this way he ranges the faithful led by their bishop on one side of a great divide. On the other stand the apostates with their lowly confederates: pagan Britons, Scotti, and Picts led by Satan.

Returning to the theme of authority in Part II, Patrick contrasts his own legitimate authority, which comes from above: from God through his consecration by the Church, with that of Coroticus, such as it was: usurped, illegitimate, and self-bestowed. He then turns from that comparison to his flock, exhorting them to have nothing to do with the apostates or their ill-gotten goods; following the exhortation with brief homilies on avarice and murder. By the end of Part II the principals on both sides, the crimes committed, and their eternal consequences have been clearly presented on a stage very like that of a Last Judgment, its backdrops lavishly adorned with Scriptural texts.

In Part III, the bishop humbly puts aside his authority to plead his case from his heart to the hearts of his hearers. How much he loves his flock is the subtext flowing beneath the brief account of all he has renounced in order to serve them. Kinship, the bonds of relationship whether fleshly or spiritual, is a theme with enormous resonance for the Irish, so Patrick's argumentation relies heavily on the "ties that bind" him to his audience, as well as on their knowledge that he forsook his own family and culture to come back to Ireland to serve them.

From this section's initial questions, which remind Patrick's audience of what prompted him to renounce his most precious human bonds, to the pointed reference to *my own* who *do not acknowledge me*, the saint's approach is personal, playing the instrument he knows is most likely to sway the Irish: kinship.

All of the previously introduced motifs are intensified in Part III, emotionally charged by the power of his personal relationship with each member of his flock; here reinforced by hope that the horror and gravity of the apostates' betrayal of their kin will be an irresistible force persuading them to return to the flock.

It ends with the plea of a beloved, but now physically weak shepherd who must depend on the music of his voice, rather than on any bodily energy, to right the wrongs he has described. He entreats the apostates based on his oneness with them, both because they have been given the same divine Father, and because they share Irishness; they by birth, he, by choice.

The final movement in Patrick's "symphony," Part IV, is gentler than Part III, relying on themes previously introduced to provide the deep chords supporting its flight from earth to Paradise; from exhortation to pure prayer. The saint has employed his gifts to the extent of his ability and now he counts on God to complete the rest of the task. Here he turns from addressing his flock on earth to imagining those who have left it so abruptly.

In Part I, Patrick had wondered who should provoke him to more grief: the victims of the crimes or the perpetrators. Now he restates his compassion for the victims only to replace it immediately with joy. The answer to the question in Part I is made even more clear here. It is for the perpetrators that he most grieves, those poor souls who have committed their crimes *for the sake of a paltry temporal realm that will undoubtedly pass away in a moment.*

For the newly baptised and their sudden entrance into eternal life he now experiences only joy. In closing, the saint prays specifically for the apostates and wishes recipients of the epistle *the peace of the Father and of the Son and of the Holy Spirit.*

Coroticus?

Who was Coroticus? *Coroticus* is the Latin form of *Ceretic*, a British name common primarily in western Wales, but also in southwestern Scotland. That it belonged to two known princes of the period in northern Wales and *All-Cluaide* (now Dumbarton, Scotland) has prompted scholars to argue for one or the other as the Coroticus of Patrick's letter.

Because there are arguments as strongly against each of these candidates as there are for them, we prefer to approach the subject differently. Historians need constantly to remind themselves that there may be more puzzle pieces left behind by time than those winnowed by previous scholars.

How many individuals bore the name *Ceretic* is evidenced by the multitude of its cognates *Caradog, Cereteg, Ceredig, Cardigan.* Despite the possibility of Coroticus' descent from a usurping family, he himself almost certainly was not a ruler since the large number of Ceretics had to far outnumber vacancies. If he were a British ruler he would not need to be living in northeastern Ireland as a predator.

When British tyrants usurped leadership positions left vacant or unsupported by departing Romans, there were many among the men of their families who did not succeed to those positions and who had to find other lines of work. It appears that our Coroticus was of the latter group – in need of employment.

Since Patrick seems to know where to send his emissaries with their letters, the attackers must have been stationed relatively nearby, somewhere in northeastern Ireland near the coast and within Patrick's *paruchia.*[78] Coroticus was an outlaw leader, probably from a fairly Romanized part of Wales where some Latin was spoken (thus farther south than Strathclyde), possibly Anglesey or the coast just south of it, then called *Ceredigion*, now Cardiganshire.

Exiled either by choice or command, Coroticus sailed with his men to the wilds of northeastern Ireland where they hoped to profit through robbery and slave-taking. From a fortified hideout they could conduct their raids and, being near the sea, could export captives easily to parts of Britain where the Irish would be unable to pursue them effectively.

We may be grateful to Coroticus, whatever his actual biography, for prompting St. Patrick to compose this epistle since, without it, we would know much less about the heart of the great man who was Ireland's apostle.

78 *Paruchia* is a term variously understood in different eras of the Irish church. In Patrick's time it referred to an area of ecclesiastical jurisdiction similar to our diocese, but with some Irish variations. For our purposes it is the area over which Patrick's episcopal authority extended. See Colman Etchingham, "The Implications of Paruchia" in *Eriu, Vol. 44* (Dublin: Royal Irish Academy, 1993) 139-162.

If Patrick was at Saul during this period (for that was where he died, and this letter was written during his final years, possibly in his last illness), Coroticus and his men may have been living near Strangford Lough with easy access to boats for the transportation of captives and plunder to Britain.

Pastoral Epistle

Part I

I Patricius, a sinner, evidently not a man of letters,[79] acknowledge myself to be an officially appointed bishop in Ireland.[80] I am convinced that what I am has been received from God,[lviii] which is why I dwell among uncultivated heathens as a convert and an exile[lix] for love of God. He is my witness that this is so.

Not that it is my choice to express myself in such a crude and blunt fashion, but the ardent love of God and the truth of Christ have stirred me up for love of those most dear [*who are*] indeed [*my*] children, on whose account I have given up homeland, relations and "my life even unto death."[lx]

Insofar as I am worthy, I live for my God to teach pagan people, even though forsaken by some.[lxi] With my own hand I have written and composed these words to be displayed, recorded, and sent to the warriors[lxii] of Coroticus. I am neither referring to "my fellow citizens," [*Romans*] nor "citizens of the Holy Romans," [*Christians*] but, on account of their evil works: "fellow citizens of demons."

As is customary with those belonging to the Enemy,[lxiii] they thrive on death, [*as*] associates of Scotti, and even of Picts and apostates,[81] [lxiv] savage murderers bloodied with the blood of innocent Christians, countless numbers of whom I have begotten in God and confirmed in Christ.

The day after the one when chrismated converts[82] in white clothing, oil still shining on their brows, were brutally massacred, slain by the swords of the previously mentioned men, I sent a letter with a holy priest whom I have taught since his baptism, along with some clerics,[lxv] so that they [*Coroticus' men and their confederates*] might relinquish something to us of the plunder or of the baptised prisoners they captured. [*In reply*] they laughed scornfully.

79 *Scilicet* "Evidently" is often used ironically. I think that is the case here. If, as it seems, this epistle was written after *Confessio* but close in time to it, the hullabaloo raised by those Gallic clerics who envied him his status as bishop and *Patricius* (considering themselves his superiors because educated in Rome) would still smart. Should any in his audience be influenced by smears about his lack of Roman legal education, Patrick emphasizes what is of much more importance: his calling received from God.

80 Since Patrick is an officially appointed bishop, his authority comes from God. As with the rest of the reasoning in this letter, the saint's status as bishop means much more to the apostates than to the Britons they assisted in attacking the newly baptised Christians.

81 See Preface to the *Pastoral Epistle* for details about the translation of this important sentence.

82 *Crismati neophyti:* "Chrismated converts" refers to the blessed oil, Holy Chrism, used to anoint new Christians after they have been immersed in the waters of baptism.

That is why I do not know for whom I should weep more: those killed or captured, or those whom the Devil has so thoroughly ensnared.[lxvi] With him the latter will be equally subjected to everlasting punishment. For "he who sins is a slave" and is called "son of the Devil," which is why every God-fearing man should keep in mind that they [*apostates, Picts, Scotti, and Britons*] are strangers to me and to Christ, my God, Whose ambassador I am.[83]

Parricide! Fratricide![lxvii] Rapacious wolves devouring the Lord's people like bread! It is written: "Demons[84] have overthrown Thy law, O Lord," which in these end times He had planted in Ireland most mercifully and opportunely, established by God's special favor.

Part II

I do not presume to exceed my authority.[lxviii] I belong among those God has called and foreordained to preach the gospel unto the ends of the earth in the face of significant persecution and despite the Enemy's envy expressed through the tyranny of Coroticus, who reveres neither God nor His chosen priests to whom He dispenses the highest divine power: "Those they bind on earth are bound also in heaven."

Therefore I beg you, holy and humble of heart,[lxix] not to flatter such men. Take neither food nor drink with them, nor give them alms until they do sufficient penance with flowing tears to God and free the servants of God and the baptised handmaidens of Christ[lxx] for whom He was crucified and died.

The Most High rejects gifts from the unjust "who offer sacrifice from the substance of the poor. They are like one who makes a sacrificial victim of a son to his father."[lxxi] It is written: "The riches which he has accumulated unjustly will be vomited from his belly. The angel of death drags him away. He

83 This sentence introduces a recurring theme, namely Patrick's relationship to the apostates, a relationship they have chosen to sever. Understanding that his personal gifts are instruments played by the Holy Spirit to attract the Irish to him, the saint employs them skillfully in order to shepherd the lost sheep back into the fold.

84 *Iniqui*, the word here translated as "demons" is an adjective in Classical Latin. When used as a plural substantive (an adjective functioning as a noun) it means "adversaries." (In Late Latin, according to Souter, *iniquus* means "the Devil.") Everything that follows serves to intensify the contrast between warriors in a battle for the souls of the Irish. On the side of God are ranged Patrick with his clerics; on the side of Satan, their chief adversary, stand Coroticus and his mercenaries along with their duplicitous Irish confederates.

will be savaged by angry dragons, killed by the adder's tongue and consumed by inextinguishable fire."

Therefore, "Woe to those who fill themselves up with what is not theirs!" or "What does it profit a man if he gains the whole world and suffers the loss of his soul?" It would take too long to discuss every instance, or to go into the whole law to select examples of such greed. Avarice is a deadly crime: "Do not covet thy neighbor's goods."

"Thou shalt not murder."[85] A murderer cannot be in Christ. "He who hates his brother is ranked a murderer," and "He who does not love his brother remains in death."[lxxii] How much more guilty is he whose hands are defiled with the blood of the children of God, whom He recently procured from the farthest corners of the earth through the prayerful petitions of our insignificance!

Part III

Can it be without God or "according to the flesh" that I came to Ireland? Who compelled me?[lxxiii]

It is by the Spirit that I am bound not to see anyone of my own kindred. Is it from myself that I have religious compassion for that pagan people who captured me and ravaged the servants and handmaidens of my father's house? According to the flesh I was born and came into the world of a decurion[86] father. But I sold my noble status. I neither blush nor regret having done so for the good of others. In short, I am a servant in Christ for that most remote pagan people on account of the ineffable glory of eternal life that is in Christ Jesus, our Lord.

85 In case any among his audience lack clarity about the two commandments at issue here: "Thou shalt not murder" and "Thou shalt not covet thy neighbor's goods," Patrick makes it abundantly clear that the criminals have broken both, gravely offending against their kindred but more profoundly, and to their eternal detriment, against their Creator, Father of the victims.

86 Here we learn that Calpurnius was a decurion, so we note that "Gildas does not mention decurions in Britain, nor is he precise in describing other officials." Christopher Snyder, *An Age of Tyrants: Britain and the Britons – A.D. 400-600,* (University Park: Penn State University Press, 1978) 115.

Constantius, in his fifth-century *Vie de Saint Germain d'Auxerre*, also lacks references to such officials in Britain. These observations add to evidence showing that Patrick could not have come from Britain, where the kind of civilian society prevalent in Gaul had not taken root, and where *civitates* were governed by officials of the Roman military, rather than by a *curia* of civilian landowners.

And if my own do not acknowledge me[87] ("a prophet has no honor in his own country") perhaps we are not from the same flock; nor do we have "one and the same God as Father."[88] As it is said: "Who is not with me is against me and who does not gather with me, scatters." We are not of one mind: "one destroys, another builds."

I neither seek what is mine nor do this for my own sake, but for God Who put this desire into my heart: that I be one of "the hunters and fishermen" He predicted for the final days.

I am envied.[lxxiv] **What shall I do, Lord?**
I am vehemently despised!

Behold Thy sheep around me, butchered
and despoiled by those aforementioned
petty mercenaries at the command of
Coroticus' hostile mind.[89]

Far from God's love is one who betrays Christians into the hands of Scotti and Picts. Rapacious wolves have divided the Lord's flock, which, through the utmost diligence, was flourishing in Ireland. For I cannot count the sons of the Scotti and daughters of kings [*who are*] monks and virgins of Christ.

To what extent does injury to the saints displease God? His displeasure reaches even unto the depths of hell. Which of the saints would not shudder to celebrate or enjoy a feast with men who have filled up their houses with the spoils of dead Christians? These live from plunder.

Wretches, they cannot recognize as poison the deadly food they give to their friends and children; just as Eve failed to understand that it was death she handed to her husband. So are all who do evil: they devote themselves to death, to eternal punishment.

It is the custom of Gallo-Roman Christians to send trustworthy, holy men to Franks and other pagans with thousands of *solidi*[90] for buying back

87 *My own* is a pointed reference to the apostates who have, as he says earlier in the letter, forsaken him.

88 *"Unum Deum Patrem"* is from the Nicene Creed and quoted twice in this section, once near the beginning and once toward the end, for emphasis.

89 As in the *Confessio*, the chiastic center of this epistle appears in boldface to highlight Patrick's perception of the central role envy plays in Coroticus' raid, just as it did at his episcopal hearing and as he now confronts it among his envious *cognati*.

90 *Solidi* were gold coins that went out of circulation early in the fifth century. Patrick's mention of them argues against those who prefer to place his life and history much later in the century.

baptised captives.[lxxv] You prefer to kill or sell them to remote pagan people ignorant of God. That is like handing over members of Christ to a brothel. What hope can you, or anyone who agrees with or flatters you, have in God?

God will judge. For it is written: "Not only those who commit evil deeds, but also those who agree with them will be condemned." I do not know what I can offer or what more I can say concerning the dead children of God who have felt the ultimate harshness of the sword. Yet, it is written: "Weep with those who weep." And again: "If one member grieves, all should grieve together."

That is why the Church "cries out, lamenting her sons and daughters"[lxxvi] whom the sword has as yet not killed but who have been sent away, exiled to far-off places where flagrant sin shamelessly and oppressively abounds. There freeborn men are placed on the market. Christians are reduced to being slaves, principally of the most shameful, most evil Picts and apostates. That is why I shall raise my voice in sadness and mourning.

O most remarkable and most beloved brethren and children whom I have begotten in Christ, so numerous I cannot count you, what can I do for you? I am able to come neither to the assistance of God nor men.[lxxvii] The irrationality of unjust men prevails over us as though we were made unrelated. Perhaps they do not believe that we have received one baptism or that we have "one and the same God as Father." To them it is dishonorable that we are Irish. Scripture says, "Do you not have the same God?" "Why has each one of you abandoned your neighbor?"[lxxviii]

Part IV

For this reason I grieve for you; I grieve, my most beloved. Yet, on the other hand, I rejoice within myself. Not for nothing have I labored nor has my exile been in vain. For though a crime so unspeakably horrendous has befallen, thanks be to God, as baptised believers you have left this world for Paradise.[91]

91 Earlier in the epistle Patrick expresses outrage and grief at the horrendous crimes perpetrated against the newest members of his flock. In this final section he puts the entire episode in perspective. He pivots abruptly from its opening words: *For this reason I grieve for you* to *I rejoice within myself.* Without diminishing the horror of what has occurred, Patrick thanks God that his baptised believers have left this world for Paradise.

[*In my mind*] I perceive you.[lxxix] You have begun to travel where there is neither night nor any more mourning or death. "But you will frisk like unfettered calves; you will trample the unjust underfoot and they will be as dust beneath your feet."

Therefore you will reign with apostles and prophets and martyrs, taking possession of eternal kingdoms as He Himself declared. He says: "They shall come from the East and from the West and will recline at table with Abraham, Isaac and Jacob in the Kingdom of Heaven."

Without are dogs and poisoners and murderers whose portion is with lying perjurers in the eternal pool of fire. Not inappropriately says the Apostle: "When the righteous are barely saved, where will the sinner and impious transgressor of the law recognize himself?"

Why then, where will Coroticus with his most detestable men, renegades against Christ, find themselves? They who distribute baptised young women as prizes for the sake of a paltry temporal realm that will undoubtedly pass away in a moment?

"Like a cloud, or smoke dispersed by the wind," deceitful sinners will perish from the presence of the Lord.[lxxx] But the holy will feast confidently with Christ, judging nations and prevailing over unjust rulers unto ages of ages. Amen.

I bear witness before God and His angels that it will be as He has revealed it to my imperfect knowledge.[lxxxi] [*These are*] not my words, but God's and the apostles' and prophets', who certainly have never lied, and which I have expressed in Latin: "He who believes will be saved, but he who does not believe will be condemned." God has spoken.

I ask, especially of any servant of God who shall volunteer to bear this letter, that it not be stolen or hidden by anyone, but rather that it be read before all the people, even in the presence of Coroticus himself.

May God inspire them [*specifically the apostates*] sometime to return to their senses and repent to Him for what they have so impiously done (murder of the brothers[92] of the Lord) that they may free the baptised women whom they captured, that they may deserve to live for God and be made whole both here and in eternity.[lxxxii]

Peace, for the sake of the Father and the Son and the Holy Spirit![lxxxiii]

92 "*Brothers*" is another witness to the murder of the men who, alive, could resist the criminals. The women, much less threatening, were to be sold.

I bind unto myself this day
the saving strength of the Trinity
by calling on Its sacred Name
the Three in One; the One in Three . . .
I bind unto myself this day
the virtues of the star-lit heavens,
white-shining moon at eventide,
the flashing of the lightning's fire,
the whirling wind's tempestuous shocks,
the firm still earth, the deep salt sea
white-hissing round the slick black rocks.
I bind unto myself this day
the power of God to raise me high;
His eye my sight, His might my strength,
His ear to hearken to my call,
The wisdom of my God to teach,
His hand to guide, His shield to ward,
the Word of God to be my speech,
His angels keeping me from harm.

After the *Lorica of St. Patrick*
Eighth century, anonymous[lxxxiv]

Chronology

387 Calpurnius Succetus is born at Tournehem in Belgica Secunda, the main Roman military base in the Bononienses, about twenty miles east-northeast of Bonaven Taberniae.

403 At about sixteen, Succetus is kidnapped from his family's estate, Enon, near Bonaven Taberniae by Scottic raiders from Ireland and becomes the slave of Milchu, chief of the Dal mBuain in Dal n'Araide near Lough Neagh.

409 Succetus escapes by ship from Ireland to Gaul and from Gaul to the Britains.

c. 412 Succetus returns to Enon to resume his place in the family. At some point not long afterward, he takes up his study of rhetoric again and enters the diaconate.

417 At the age of thirty, Calpurnius Succetus is ordained deacon by Amator, bishop of Auxerre, perhaps receiving the name of Magonus at this time. He goes to Lerins for spiritual formation and theology, either now or a little later.

418 St. Amator dies and Germanus is ordained bishop of Auxerre some time afterward.

424 Magonus returns to Bononia as deacon to serve the bishop there and oversee his family estate.

429 According to some, Magonus accompanies Bishops Germanus and Lupus to Maxima Caesarensis in the Britains when they sail there from Bononia to combat Pelagianism on the island.

432 At forty-five, Magonus is ordained bishop by Germanus, bishop of Auxerre who sends him to the Christians of Leinster in Ireland and, once that community has been secured in faith, he then travels to the pagans of Ulster. If the saint did not receive this agnomen (Magonus) as a deacon, he must have received it at episcopal ordination.

439 Auxilius, Secundinus, and Iserninus, having been ordained bishops in Gaul, are sent back to Leinster to continue Patrick's work there while he concentrates his efforts on the Ulster pagans.

441 According to the *Annals of Ulster* "Patricius the bishop *probatus est* in the catholic faith" by Pope Leo I. The *Annals of Inisfallen* has *"Probatio sancti Patricii in fide catolica"* under the same year.[lxxxv]

c. 460 Magonus is elevated to Patricius by the emperor, almost certainly Majorian. Some time afterward, his newly baptised Christians are slaughtered and abducted by Coroticus' men. He writes both of his surviving epistles during this period.

465 At about seventy-eight, Patricius dies at Saul and is buried there. Under the year 552, the *Annals of Ulster* record the information from the lost *Book of Cuanu* that Colmcille had a shrine constructed for Patrick's relics.

Endnotes

i The "Scribe's Poem" is a free version of one of several poems ascribed to St. Colmcille (Columba) until analysis revealed them to be much later compositions. This one is from the eleventh or twelfth century.

ii I may differ in perception and conclusions from those of greater erudition, but I do so with the grateful recognition that my efforts could not have been undertaken without theirs. Reasons and documentation for these differences will be found in *I, Patricius: The Roman History of an Irish Saint* as well as, to a lesser extent, here in the notes. May those who come after forgive any errors and may this small contribution to the corporate enterprise on St. Patrick's behalf be worth the effort of correcting them!

iii For more details about Patrick's homeland and birthplace and why Britain *could not* have been his patria as well as why Gaul *was*, see chapters II and IV of *I, Patricius* "An Irritating Subject" and "None of the Above" respectively. That *Bonaven Taberniae*, the place of the saint's kidnapping and of his grandfather's church, was the *vicus* of *Bononia* (Boulogne) in Gaul is well attested by many sources ancient and modern, in Latin, Irish, and French, as well as in English.

Probus, the tenth-century Irish scholar, places *Bonaven Taberniae*, in *Nevtria (Neustria)* the Merovingian Frankish designation for the province which, by the time Probus was writing, had included *Bonaven/Bononia/Boulogn*e for about five hundred years. *Genair Patraicc*, an even older source asserts that the saint was born in *Nevtria,* followed by several other early witnesses.

This subject has been complicated by some writers' confounding Patrick's birthplace with that of his kidnapping, by the isolation of the British Isles from the Continent after the Merovingian conquest, and by the confusion of the nouns *Brito* (someone from Brittany or a French Britain), with *Britannus* (someone from Britain) and *Britannicus* (British, meaning from the island of Britain), an adjective. Subtleties and distinctions regarding these words have also been overlooked. This is more fully explored in *I, Patricius.*

iv *Goidelic* was a more ancient form of Celtic language, spoken in the most intensely Gaulish of Roman provinces in Gaul: *Gallia Lugdunensis.* From there it was brought to Ireland, sometime between 1000 and 600 BC, where it became the basis for the Irish and Scottish languages (the Irish brought it to Scotland). *Brythonic* was the primary form of Celtic spoken wherever Britons predominated, and formed the basis of Welsh, Cornish and Breton.

v I differ with Dr. Howlett's divisions between **Exodus** and **Leviticus**, and between **Leviticus** and **Numbers**. I end **Exodus** in the middle of (Chapter 25), beginning **Leviticus** with the second half of (25). Dr. Howlett begins **Exodus** with (Chapter 26). I end **Leviticus** after (Chapter 34), beginning **Numbers** with (Chapter 35). Dr. Howlett begins **Numbers** with the last two lines of (Chapter 37).

Because Patrick's anacoluthic biblical quotations are shaped by his epistles' literary and chiastic requirements, he may not have been as strictly numerical with regard to chiasms as Dr. Howlett believes. Thus, analogies with the Pentateuch and other literary considerations may have occasionally triumphed over the rigidity of adhering to chiasms when meaning was at issue.

Ending **Exodus** with the relation of Patrick's mystical experience and beginning **Leviticus** with the statement that the Lord is his advocate seems a more graceful transition and more in keeping with the two biblical books these sections mimic.

Similarly, with regard to the transition from **Leviticus** to **Numbers**, Patrick has made a concluding statement in **Leviticus** when he says that the gospel has been proclaimed to the farthest corners of the earth. He seems to be launching into **Numbers** at Chapter (35) in Bieler's text with his desire not to bore readers by enumerating too many of his labors.

Dr. Howlett (*op. cit.* 12-13) describes the mechanism of Patrick's chiastic composition best:

> We may take as a model for such composition the vision of the Prophet Ezechiel, a captive, like Patrick, in a foreign land, where he saw *et aspectus earum et opera quasi si rota in medio rotae* 'both their appearance and working as if it were a wheel in the middle of a wheel,' like the inclusion of a chiastic sentence within a chiastic paragraph, itself within a chiastic chapter which is within a chiastic whole.

The ancients employed chiasm in narration and writing, most notably in Homer's *Iliad* and *Odyssey* and in the Hebrew and Christian scriptures. For our purposes it helps to understand that progression through a chiastic text is not so much linear, as circular or spiraling, meaning revealing itself at the center of chiasms rather than through the beginning, middle, and end form of development with which we are most familiar. Thus we will find the most significant sentences for interpretation of St. Patrick's epistles at the centers of chiasms.

How extraordinarily, technically, and mathematically Patrick structured his epistles can be glimpsed in Dr. Howlett's and Dr. Maire de Paor's expositions of them. An added benefit of employing this technique is that, despite the tendency of humans to err, such ancient texts can be transmitted, and in some cases accurately reconstructed, with reference to their chiastic patterns.

vi *Conf.* (10) is the source of our understanding that Patrick had begun his rhetorical studies before the kidnapping interrupted them.

vii See Bieler, *op. cit.* 34, who says, "It is often the most intelligent and conscientious scribes that go farthest in biblical standardization. Patrick's bible text was partly Old Latin, partly Vulgate, and partly a transitional version, but the earlier elements are not preserved in all MSS, and not always in the best ones."

One may apply Bieler's insight to a broader classification of scribes in the sense that many errors other than those of biblical standardization are attributable to "intelligent and conscientious" copyists who, ironically, might have served us better had they been less intelligent and simply copied what they received.

viii I capitalize "Patricius" throughout the text because it is a rank as well as a name, and in order not to seesaw visually between the name of our saint and his rank. This is also to distinguish his Patrician rank from the patrician class of the early Roman Republic.

ix See also Gertrude Mesmer, "The Cult of Saint Patrick in the Vicinity of Drackenstein" in *Journal of the Armagh Diocesan Historical Society, Vol. 4, No. 2* (Armagh: Cumann Seanchais Ard Mhacha, 1961-62) 68-75.

Before Saint Patrick

x These two poems are included to give a sense of the Ireland to which St. Patrick came. The first, attributed to Amergin, the primordial druidic brehon and poet of the Sons of Mil, was found in an eleventh-century mythological compilation called *Leabhar Gabala* or *Book of Invasions*, but it includes material that is much earlier. We don't know how old the poem actually is, but it, like the early mythological cycles, exudes the air of pre-Christian Ireland.

"Magh Slecht" purports to describe the adoration of *Cromm Cruaich*, the main deity of pre-Christian Ireland. While *Cromm Cruaich* is mentioned neither by St. Patrick, nor by Tigernach or Muirchu, the saint's earliest "biographers," strong early traditions connect the saint with *Magh Slecht* (Plain of Adoration or Prostrations) where the idol was worshipped near Ballymagauran in County Cavan.

Patrick's destruction of the idol is recounted in a *Dindshenchas* (lore of places or place names) poem in the twelfth-century *Book of Leinster* and in the ninth-century *Tripartite Life*, where the idol is called *Cern Cruach*. It appears to be identical to *Kerman Kelstach*, considered god of all Ulster, whose sanctuary was at Clogher in County Tyrone. Both these sun deities were stone covered with gold. Clogher (*Cloch-Oir*) means "gold stone." For a little more about Cromm Cruaich, see *The Annals of Ireland by the Four Masters*, Vol. I, 43.

Confessio

xi *Confessio*, the word Patrick uses to describe this epistle at the end of it, does not mean "confession" as we ordinarily understand it. It means "testimony," "witness," or, in Late Latin, "acknowledgment of God." It has legal overtones, continuing the subliminal image of a court running through the entire letter. A category of Christian saints is called "confessors" because their distinguishing characteristic is their public witness to Christ.

Genesis

xii *Bonaven Taberniae* was the oldest section, or vicus, of Bononia, having developed from *Gesoriacum*, the marine *oppidum*, or fort, of the *Gesoriaci*, a tribe of the *Morini*, a maritime people who lived in the area when Julius Caesar came in 56 BC and who still formed the basis of the native population in the fifth century. "... about the reign of Constantine the Great [early fourth century] the Celtic name *Bonaven* or *Bonaun*, alias *Bonon*, [*Rivermouth*] which was latinized to *Bononia*, became more general." (Lanigan, *op. cit.* p. 93.)

The word *Bonaven/Bunaven/Bonavem* is Celtic, composed of *bon/bun* and *aven*: river. *Bon/bun* means "root, foundation," or, in the case of a river, "mouth." If one imagines a tree with roots at its base and branches growing from its trunk, it is easy to understand the Celtic transference of *bun/bon* to the mouth of a river.

Like a tree, a river spreads at its base (or mouth). Invisible tributaries flow like roots stretching into the sea, and little streams, like branches, grow out of the river on either side as one proceeds upstream. *Aven/aun/on* means river or water and *Bononia* is the Latinized form of *Bunaven/Bonaven*, or *Bonon*. See also Jean Baptiste Bullet, "Dictionnaire Celtique" in *Memoires sur la langue celtique, t. III* (Besancon: chez Cl. Joseph Daclin, Imprimeur du Roi, 1754) 104 or Nicholas Cardinal Wiseman, *The Dublin Review, Vol. 100* (London: W. Spooner, etc., 1887) 352.

Boulogne's upper city, Bononia proper, was built on the heights above the *Fretum Gallicanum*, also called *Fretum Bononicum* (later, the Straits of Dover or Pas de Calais) the narrowest part of the English Channel. The upper city first contained barracks for men of the Classis Britannica, so named, not for the island of Britain as many suppose, but for the Brythonic people who dwelt on and controlled both sides of the Channel or the *Mare Britannicus.*

Muir n'Icht, the Celtic name for the Channel, seems to have been named after the Celtic name for the Isle of Wight: *Icht*. Since the earliest written mentions of the island are in Diodorus Siculus (first century BC), and they refer to it as *Ictis*, it would appear that the Romans had simply Latinized the old Celtic name, calling the island *Vectis*. They called the port at Bononia, *Portus Iccius,* and there are references to *Mare Iccium* or Iccian Sea in early Latin writers.

The best account of the etymology of the name that I have been able to find is in William Henry Davenport Adams, *The History, Topography, and Antiquities of the Isle of Wight* (London: Smith, Elder and Co.: 1856) 223. Adams' more learned exposition contradicts earlier theorists: Sir Christopher Hawkins in *Observations on the Tin Trade of the Ancients in Cornwall and on the "Ictis" of Diodorus Siculus* (1811) and Robert Wallace in "On the Ictis of Diodorus Siculus" (1844). These both suffer from the assumption that *Ictis* was Greek and go into a learned discussion based on that error. Also see Lanigan, *op. cit.* 139 for a little about the area with reference to the death of *Niall Noigiallach.*

It may be that *Iccius*, an influential ambassador from the Gaulish *Remi* to Julius Caesar, was the catalyst for the critical alliance of that tribe with the Romans, and naming the Bononian port for Iccius, a way of further securing the allegiance between Caesar and the Remigian Celts. Extremely influential among the Gauls, the Remi were one of the only tribes who did not join Vercingetorix in rebelling against Caesar. Iccius lived in the first century BC.

xiii *Enim* is the common rendering of a word that must have looked different in early manuscripts since Sir James Ware has *Enon* in his seventeenth-century edition of St. Patrick's epistles. I have preferred this variant, as did most nineteenth-century commentators on Patrick's letters, because *enim* is not grammatical in the sentence and is destructive of meaning. It implies causation, which does not make sense in context. Aware that there was no *enon* in Latin, early transcribers must have substituted the ungrammatical *enim* for the Celtic compound word *enon*.

Potitus was not a priest from Bonaven Taberniae *because* (*enim* means *for* in the sense of causation) he had a small estate nearby from which Patrick was taken captive, as many have translated the sentence. Patrick's being kidnapped nearby post-dated his grandfather's origins in Bonaven Taberniae or his undertaking service at the church, and could not have been the cause of his doing so.

On the other hand, if the period is placed so that we understand proximity of his estate to Bonaven Taberniae to be the reason why Potitus served as priest there, we are left with *ubi ego capturam dedi* (*where I was taken captive*) dangling as an incomplete sentence. Placing a full stop after *Bonaven Taberniae* and making another sentence of *Villulam Enon prope habuit ubi ego capturam dedi* (Nearby he had an estate, "Enon," where I was taken captive.) restores both grammar and meaning.

Where I was taken captive (*ubi capturam dedi*) literally translated is *where I conceded capture*. Patrick uses the same phrase again in reference to his being made a captive by the pirates who brought him back to Gaul. Because he is so careful in his choice of words, one wonders if he is not saying that at some point he had a choice in the matter. Perhaps each time the other option was unpalatable, but it was a choice nevertheless, most likely between captivity and death. If so, in "conceding capture" he chose life.

Those twentieth-century scholars quick to assume that Patrick was incapable of clear or grammatical expression might not find such ineptitude (i.e. non sequiturs or dangling clauses) disturbing. But the saint's ability elsewhere in the epistle to communicate concisely and with mathematical precision removes such a rendering from the realm of possibility, confirming *Enon* as the actual word.

xiv *Our bishops:* Many translate *sacerdotibus* "to our priests" but Patrick's use of *presbyter* in the preceding sentence to describe his grandfather demonstrates that he would have used the same word in this instance if he had meant "priest." Furthermore, ". . . the ordinary and general use of the word *sacer-*

dos within the period referred to [*the fourth and mid-fifth centuries*] and, indeed, for many years later, is to signify a bishop . . ." See John Dowden, D.D., F.S.A."Observations and Conjectures on the Kirkmadrine Epigraphs" at journals.socantscot.org./index.php/psas/article/download/6705/6674, p. 252.

Since *civitates* in the Rheims diocese (each having a bishop) included both capitals of the Morini: Bonaven and Tarvanna (Therouanne), and both cities had bishops, this can explain Patrick's use of bishops in the plural.

Another possibility is that Patrick is referring to the metropolitan bishop at Rheims and his suffragan at Bononia. See Van Drival, *Histoire des Eveques de Boulogne,* (Boulogne-sur-Mer: Berger freres, 1865) 3-45, for the early history of the See of Boulogne from AD 270 to the seventh-century establishment of Therouanne as the see for the entire area, under St. Omer. Also see Antoine Auguste Bruzen de la Martiniere, *Le grand dictionnaire geographique, historique, et critique, Tome II* (Paris: Libraires Associes, 1768) 61 for a list of the *Metropolis Civitas Remorum*, which includes suffragan bishops of the metropolis of Rheims in Belgica Secunda, showing bishops for both Bononia and Tarvanna.

xv The Latin for "windstorm of His living Spirit" is *iram animationis suae*. Patrick is describing the living Divine Spirit (*animationis suae*) symbolically manifest as a wind-like power that scatters the faithless youths and disperses them among unbelievers. *Iram* is "wrath, anger, fury," It calls to mind the phrase from Psalm 68 sung repeatedly during Orthodox Pascha: "Let God arise; let His enemies be scattered."

xvi *Ubi nunc parvitas mea esse videtur inter alienigenas* is the Latin for this phrase which appears to mean that Patrick's dwelling among foreigners was viewed by some Gallo-Roman clerics, whose ideas of greatness remained mired in worldliness, as an indication of his unimportance. Had Patrick been bishop of an important metropolitan see in Gaul they might have better understood his elevation to Patricius, but they were incapable of appreciating the bestowal of this honor on someone laboring outside the empire among people they considered barbaric.

xvii *This is why I cannot be silent* . . . This paragraph, just preceding Patrick's creed, is very significant. It alludes to *such a great conferring of privileges* and *such great grace* (being made Patricius with all the honors that accompany elevation), which he has received *in the land of my captivity.* The Latin word *beneficium* refers to a privilege, promotion, or favor conferred for service to the public. *Gratia* in Late Latin means *blessing* or *grace*, most particularly a favor or grace bestowed by God.

The saint is establishing the first and most obvious reason for the epistle, as well as attributing the honor he has received to God's favor. Taking his own advice about the best way to show his gratitude, Patrick immediately continues with a formal statement of his faith. Not far from the end of the *Confessio*, in **Deuteronomy** (55) he echoes this paragraph, referring again to his being *exalted beyond measure by the Lord,* despite his awareness of unworthiness.

xviii This is the beginning of a creed ending with "Trinity of holiness" possibly derived from the Gallican liturgical rites Patrick brought with him from Gaul. A transitional form of the ancient Eucharistic rite and of the *Hours*, used in Gaul, the Gallican Liturgy was a bridge between the eastern rites from which it developed and the later western rite.

xix *Obedientes*, here rendered "receptive," is commonly translated "obedient, compliant, dutiful," In this context Patrick is speaking of obedience to the Holy Spirit as a prerequisite for becoming a child of God; an obedience that means "receptivity" if we consider receptivity an aspect of compliance, of a listening faith bearing fruit in action conformable (obedient) to the instruction of the Holy Spirit.

xx After the creed are two scriptural quotes. The second, *"Moreover, to explain and praise the works of the Lord bestows honor"* is followed by *So, despite the fact that I am imperfect in many respects, I also desire my "brethren and peers" to know my nature that they may be able to perceive the dedication of my life.* For the word here translated as *peers*, Patrick employs the word *cognatus*.

In using *cognatus*, Patrick is not referring to his relatives (recall that *parens* is the word he uses for them) but to those who share a common background as Romans and clerics, his colleagues or peers still in Gaul. For the Irish mission was generated in Gaul and it still maintained strong links with the Gallic church which continued to supply clerics for it.

The saint's use of *brethren and peers* (*fratribus et cognatis*) is a prime example of the original context of a quote (i.e. its biblical context) bestowing more meaning on the sentence in which it occurs. For the biblical original refers to betrayers, and among Patrick's *fratribus et cognatis* were his own betrayers. (See **Leviticus** for more on that episode). If "modern readers have paid more attention to what is apparently said than to what is really meant," (Howlett, *op. cit.* 102) postmodern readers now have the tools to attend more profoundly and accurately to Patrick's entire meaning. Also see Howlett, *op. cit.* 97 for more on the biblical context for Patrick's use of *cognatis*.

That the reference to *brethren and peers* is followed immediately by a short section on lying, near the end of **Genesis** and just before the ***Apologia***, is not accidental. At about the same distance from the end of the epistle, at the beginning of **Deuteronomy**, we find a chiastic parallel: another short section about lying. Patrick has been slandered, primarily by his *fratribus et cognatis*, but he does not accuse them. Rather he directs impersonal reflections on the consequences of lying toward himself, should he be guilty of that sin. His audience is well able to absorb any implications for themselves.

xxi Patrick's ***Apologia***, which explains both why he is writing now and why he did not do so earlier, offers many insights into the saint's character and personality. On the one hand, he is aware that the scriptural models influencing and shaping his verbal expression are not those shaping the literary output of his peers in Gaul. On the other, he knows his capabilities and that, despite early obstacles to his rhetorical education, he composes his letters with considerable dexterity. He acknowledges all of this with wonder, attributing his elevation to the episcopacy and to the rank of Patricius, as well as any verbal virtuosity he may exhibit, to God's graciousness.

xxii *The process by which my language was shaped:* The Old Latin Bible and other biblical versions, not works of secular literature which most Gallic stylists imitated, were the primary models for the development of Patrick's style: the antiphonal arrangement of phrases, the chiastic structure of his epistles. His quotes too are from every book of the Bible. This departure from common literary practice was deliberate, not due to ignorance as some twentieth-century Patrician scholars assert.

xxiii ... *my sins prevented my mastering what I studied then* establishes that Patrick had started his rhetorical studies, ordinarily begun at age fifteen, when his kidnapping interrupted them. He has already attributed his capture to his sins of unbelief, and failure to pay attention to the bishops. For more about education in Late Antiquity, see Henri Irenee Marrou, *Histoire de l'education dans l'antiquite, Vol. 2* (Paris: Editions du Seuil, 1981) 218ff. and 389ff., and M. L. Clarke, *Higher Education in the Ancient World* (London/New York: Routledge, 2012).

At the time of his kidnapping, Patrick would have completed elementary studies with a grammaticus and just begun the study of rhetoric in preparation for a career serving the empire as a decurion, since, at that time he had not thought of serving the church and he had inherited his father's position as a decurion. Many references in the *Confessio* demonstrate Patrick's expectation of studying *the way others did*, and his regret that his kidnapping postponed some of these studies and precluded others (e.g. legal).

Both the construction of the epistles and the fact that he became a deacon and later, a bishop, certify that Patrick undertook rhetorical studies after his return to Gaul, but he also makes it plain that he did not pursue the study of secular and ecclesiastical law in Rome as did others in the Gallic episcopacy. For more on this subject, see Jill Harries, *Law and Empire in Late Antiquity* (Cambridge: Cambridge University Press, 1999) and a dissertation by Maria Edith Doerfler, *Law and Order: Monastic Formation, Episcopal Authority, and Conceptions of Justice in Late Antiquity* (dukespace.lib.duke.edu/dspace, 2013).

xxiv *Propter retributionem* is the Latin that is literally translated *on account of retribution or punishment* which, in context, would mean *criticism*. Because this sentence has a few anacoluthic biblical quotes it is difficult to translate gracefully.

xxv At this point in the ***Apologia*** Patrick takes a formal tone as he recognizes the great lords of the Church in his audience. Part IV (**Numbers**) is the counterpoint to this section, when his tone becomes intimate and personal as he addresses his fellow clerics in Ireland, urging them to remain faithful to the task and to *do more powerful deeds*. Patrick's continental peers, as well as the clergy in Ireland, require a clear accounting before the saint dies and there is no one else to give it. The fact that his Gallic *cognati* form part of his intended audience suggests that news of his elevation as Patricius had stirred up old rumors from the time of the hearing before his episcopal ordination, making this clarification not only timely, but necessary for them.

Patrick has previously specified the continental audience for whom he is writing: primarily his brethren and peers in Gaul. *Opto "fratribus et cognatis" meis scire qualitatem meam*. Now he addresses them as *you great and lowly who fear God* and *you clever masters of rhetoric*. Among his brethren and peers are those rhetorical masters of whose cleverness the saint is only too painfully aware, for we may recall that the context of the biblical quotation from which he takes *brethren and peers* lets us know that some of his betrayers are among them.

The saint asks everyone, including those who are *clever masters of rhetoric*, to join him in amazement at the height to which he *who was neither worthy nor so distinguished* has been elevated *from the midst of those who appear to be wise and learned in the law, powerful in discourse and all affairs.* Why has this amazing thing happened? Because *He* [God] *inspired me before others in this abominable world to be one who, with awe and reverence and without complaint, should faithfully go to that pagan people onto whom Christ's love engrafted me.*

Patrick is subtly evoking astonishment that a person considered neither a rhetorician, nor well-versed in law like many of his addressees was chosen before those possessing such attributes to undertake the mission to the Irish and is now being supremely honored for the success of that mission. In doing this, he is mirroring the amazement of many of his *cognati.*

As if that were not enough, wonder of wonders, such an individual, isolated for three decades from any society able to burnish his literary expression, is sufficiently sophisticated to produce this letter, intricately structured as it is. Such skill he attributes to the grace of God tutoring him, certain that his weaknesses and limitations manifest God's power and glory more than if all his accomplishments could be attributable to him alone.

It is only near the end of **Numbers**, (47), that we understand that the epistle is also being addressed to the saint's fellow clerics in Ireland and, at the conclusion of **Deuteronomy**, Patrick shows that he realizes that others beyond the circle of addressees in Ireland and on the Continent may read his testimony at some point: *whoever will have thought it worthwhile to read or digest this writing.*

xxvi His **Apologia** ends with: *I was neither so worthy nor so distinguished that the Lord should grant this to his servant – after labors and such burdens, after imprisonment, after many years among that pagan people – that He should freely bestow such a great blessing on me for which I neither hoped in my youth nor thought about at any time.* The *great blessing* is his elevation to *Patricius*, which he doesn't need to name, having just described being *elevated to the top of the house* and *raised up . . . from the midst of those who appear wise and learned in law*, and since the entire epistle is his formal response to that honor.

How late in his life the honor was bestowed is demonstrated by: *after many labors and such burdens, after imprisonment, after many years among that pagan people.* After all these years of arduous labor in a far away vineyard, Patrick is stunned that in old age he should be granted an honor beyond his wildest dreams, *for which I neither hoped in my youth nor thought about at any time.*

Exodus

xxvii The Voice is not referring to a religious fast, but to the limited rations provided Patrick as a slave. It merely states that it is fortuitous that Patrick is physically prepared for privations he will endure on the arduous journey ahead.

xxviii The second time Patrick refers to the Voice, he uses the word *responsum* (answer) instead of *vox*. I translate it as Voice for clarity in English, but Patrick's word tells us that the second time the Voice spoke to him was in response to his own question about how he was to accomplish his escape.

Since the ship Patrick finds waiting for him at *Inbher De* (Arklow) went to Gaul, this confirms Gaul as his *patria*. The saint never suggests he was not taken to his *patria*.

xxix For an idea of one kind of boat that was commonly in use at the time, see online images of the Broighter boat, a miniature in gold of a type of curragh with sails, a mast with a yardarm, fifteen oars, nineteen oarlocks and room for eighteen oarsmen. Because this boat was part of a hoard discovered in County Derry that includes items from the "last half-century BC," Peter Harbison speculates that it may have belonged to the *Veneti*, sea-faring Celts from Brittany fleeing from Caesar in 56 BC. See Peter Harbison, *Pre-Christian Ireland* (London: Thames and Hudson, 1988) 176.

The hoard might also be a stash of plunder obtained by raiding Scotti, which they had been unable to retrieve, perhaps because they were killed before an opportunity to do so presented itself. This kind of boat may have been among those in the pirate fleet that brought Patrick to Ireland for it is not unlike many in use for centuries afterward, even to the present day. Some in the fleet could even have been Roman ships captured by the Irish or left behind when the Romans left Britain.

xxx Manuscripts differ as to whether the men had *eaten their fill of meat* or *their dogs were replenished.* I chose the "Paris" manuscript version (tenth century, found in Compiegne, Picardy), putative parent to the Cottonian and Oxford manuscripts: *carne eorum repleti sunt*, rather than *canes eorum repleti sunt.*

Patrick makes no reference to dogs as cargo, and, since these men were Irish pirates, it is unlikely that they would have been burdening themselves with legitimate merchandise with which to trade in Gaul, especially the kind that required feeding; to say nothing of the difficulty of herding dogs overland for a month when they themselves were on short rations. Patrick states that many of the men had fainted and been left behind half-dead. Thus one wonders why, if indeed they had dogs with them they didn't kill some for food rather than leaving men behind to die.

xxxi Writing in old age, the saint marvels that he was inspired to call upon Elias, the favorite prophet of both Jews and early Christians, when he would have been ignorant of the prophet in his irreligious youth. He is struck by the convergence of the Greek name for sun, *helios*, with *Helia* (Elias) as he is with the coincidence of the rising sun with his deliverance from depression. The mysterious nature of this experience is deepened by Patrick's expressed conviction in *Conf.* (60) that the material sun is an icon of the true Sun, Jesus Christ.

xxxii *The Britains* refers to areas occupied by British or Brythonic tribes and its meaning varies with the period in which it occurs. Very early on the term referred to coastal areas of northern Gaul inhabited by British tribes as well as to the island of Great Britain. As time went on, the term gradually became almost exclusively restricted to the island. Then, after the Roman division of the island into provinces, *the Britains* usually referred to those provinces.

During Patrick's lifetime and long after his death, *Armorica*, which included *Bononia*, was referred to as *Britannia* by writers. A map drawn by Le Brue depicting Gaul before Caesar shows Britons occupying Normandy, Picardy and parts of the Straits of Calais (*Fretum Gallicanum* near Boulogne). See Martin A. O'Brennan, *Ancient Ireland: her Milesian chiefs etc.* (Dublin: John Mulaney, 1865) 71.

xxxiii The statement *received me as the son*, even if translated as *a son* (insertion of the article is left to translators, of whom most have inserted "a") makes no sense if Patrick is returning to his own parents. Of course they would receive him as their long-lost son! Instead, he is referring to acknowledgement by his relatives as *the* son of his father in the sense of taking on hereditary responsibilities and receiving back his rights.

These would include the management of the Calpurnius property in the absence of his father. This is made even more certain when we see that, as bishop, he is able to dispose of that property. He never makes reference to siblings.

xxxiv Manuscripts vary as to whether the man in Patrick's dream bearing letters from Ireland was called *Victoricus* or *Victoricius*. Aware that, late in the fourth century, St. Victricius of Rouen had undertaken a mission to evangelize the Morini around Bononia, some scribes must have decided that "Victoricus" was an earlier scribal error – and corrected it – thus the "Victoricius manuscripts."

I prefer the Victoricus manuscripts because Victoricus is the name of a saint with even closer ties to Patrick than Victricius the former bishop of Rouen, being, as mentioned, not only the original evangelist of the Boulonnais, but the founder of the church served by Patrick's father and grandfather and probably the one in which he was baptised.

See Jacques Malbrancq, *Morinis Morinorum Rebus Tome i*, (Tournai: Adrianus Quinque, 1639) 128. Malbrancq describes the coming of Sts. Fuscianus and Victoricus to Bononia, where they established its first Christian church c. 270 with Victoricus as its bishop. Also in *Tome i*, the *Chronologia* has several listings referring to the careers of Fuscianus and Victoricus in *Tarvanna* and *Bononia*. Malbrancq's work is valuable primarily for information gleaned from Latin and French sources no longer available to us. He also uses early Irish sources without being able to critically evaluate them so, in places, his work exhibits the same patchwork quality as theirs.

The church St. Victoricus founded at the end of the third century, Patrick's grandfather's church, was originally a house church and one of the "numerous small churches erected in Gaul through the second half of the fourth century onwards" after Constantine legitimized Christianity throughout the Empire. See Anthony King, *Roman Gaul and Germany,* (London: British Museum Press, 1990) 192.

Today, having been several times rebuilt on the same site, it is called *Notre Dame de Saint Sang* after some twelfth-century relics, including one with blood stains thought to be those of Christ, sent by Godefroy de Bouillon, Comte de Boulogne, from Jerusalem to his mother, Comtesse Ide de Lorraine, also Comtesse de Boulogne, who frequently came there to pray. The chapel was "situated near the sea, at some distance from the walls of the ancient Bononia."

The mouth of the Liane was quite a bit wider in the Late Roman Empire. If one follows the route of the *ancien rivage* (ancient riverbank) now marked by a small street of that name, one may see that Potitus' church originally sat close to the riverbank where it would have served the families of the Classis Britannica.

xxxv *Sancte puer* is usually rendered "holy boy," but it cannot be correct for this context. *Puer* may mean "child" or "bachelor." Thus, since Patrick is twenty-four or twenty-five, well beyond *pueritia* which ended at fourteen, "bachelor" or "young man" is more appropriate. *Sanctus* means "sacred" or "holy" but also "incorrupt," "without vices," "chaste." As Patrick became a man of prayer, his lack of vices might impress even people who would not recognize holiness. He could recognize himself as a chaste young man but not a "holy boy." On the contrary, he viewed his boyhood as unbelieving and sinful.

xxxvi That he impressed the Irish during his captivity and perhaps had even begun evangelization among them, seems probable because Patrick finds a dream credible that portrays his former Irish associates addressing him as *chaste young man* while calling him to return. He attributes the fact that the Lord made things happen as the Irish wished, to their "loud calling" or "invocation" (*clamos, clamoris*) as though in answer to prayer.

See R.A.S. Macalister, "Silva Focluti" in *Journal of the Royal Society of Antiquaries of Ireland 7th Series, Vol. 2, No. 1* (Dublin: Royal Society of Antiquaries of Ireland, 1932) 26 for the reasoning behind his translation "come and help us" rather than "come and walk with us" – with which I agree.

Leviticus

xxxvii The opening sentences of this section remind us of the saint's experience of the indwelling of the Holy Spirit at the end of **Exodus**, attributing delivery from the trials he is about to experience to that indwelling and to the pleading of his Advocate within him and on his behalf. This sudden change from a state of mystical prayer at the end of **Exodus** to being attacked at his episcopal hearing in **Leviticus** is meant to allow the reader to share Patrick's shock at his betrayal by his best friend. Like the biblical book, Patrick's **Leviticus** deals with religio-legal preparation for entry into the "Promised Land," which in this case is Ireland rather than Canaan, the future land of Israel.

The transition from **Exodus** to **Leviticus** is the first of two places in the epistle where my "Pentateuchal" divisions differ from those of Dr. Howlett. I end **Exodus** just before line 149 (25) with the end of his spiritual experience and its revelation of the Holy Spirit, beginning **Leviticus** at line 149: *In this way I have learned by experience* followed by his reflection on the Holy Spirit and his acknowledgment that the Holy Spirit was his *Advocate.*

The Holy Spirit's role as his counselor is being subtly contrasted with that of his treacherous *defensor*. This allusion makes a better transition to the legal section of the epistle than the too abrupt beginning: *When tried by some of my elders* . . . See also endnote v.

In **Leviticus** we learn that Patrick was a deacon who became a bishop according to the custom of fifth-century Gaul because, as in earlier Christian centuries, deacons were ordained to serve the bishop, the diaconate functioning as a quasi-novitiate for the episcopate. In this period the overwhelming majority of bishops of Rome were not priests before their elevation, but became bishops after serving as deacons. Neither Germanus nor Palladius was a priest before becoming bishop.

Questions concerning the way Patrick functioned liturgically are not easy to answer because the information we have about the liturgical functioning of fifth-century bishops is blurry and probably reflects a lack of uniformity in practice. Theologically, a bishop possessed the fullness of priesthood, but what that entailed liturgically in the fifth century is simply unclear. One source supplying some information about relations between bishops and deacons is the third-century *Didascalia Apostolorum I–VI.*

Early *Lives* and the majority of scholars establish Patrick in Auxerre under Bishop Germanus for his diaconate, where he underwent at least part of his clerical preparation for orders and where his episcopal hearing was held; experiences he views as analogous to the biblical *Leviticus*. While this section is more obviously concerned with law and legalities, being centered on Patrick's ecclesiastical hearing, a careful reader of the epistle (especially in Latin) will note that law is frequently referenced throughout the entire epistle. One senses that there is much more to learn from a thorough investigation of this aspect of the *Confessio*.

xxxviii *Sed Dominus pepercit proselito et peregrino propter nomen suum benigne* is translated here as *Yet the Lord spared a convert, alien for the sake of His own gracious being* . . . Others translate it *Yet the Lord spared a sojourner and exile on account of His own kindly name.* What has been said elsewhere (footnote 23) about *nomen* meaning *being* holds here.

Proselitus, a noun, refers to a newcomer, particularly in the sense of a convert, as from heathenism to Judaism or Christianity. Patrick cannot be referring to himself as a newcomer to Gaul since he was about to be made a bishop and had been back in Gaul for around twenty years. Recall that he is now forty-five, having returned from "the Britains" when he was twenty-four or twenty-five. But he was a convert from unbelief to faith, soon to return voluntarily to alien status for the sake of spreading the gospel.

Peregrinus, an adjective or a substantive (the noun is *peregrinitas*) means "foreign" or "alien," ("foreigner" or "alien" if used as a substantive). In the diaconate Patrick was alien in two senses. He had been removed from the Roman world at a young age, returning to it with perspectives not shared by those who had never lived outside its frontiers. In addition, his unusual life experience and the postponement of his rhetorical education, making him about nine years older than those with whom he studied, would have given both Patrick and those around him a sense that he was different, a bit foreign.

xxxix *from my baptism: Infantia* is usually translated "infancy" or "childhood" but may also refer to baptism or to "that age at which boys used to be dedicated to the clerical state." (Lanigan, *op. cit.* 300, n. 104.) In this instance *infantia* does not refer to dedication to the clerical state, but whether Patrick means from infancy or from baptism is neither clear nor an important distinction, since he would almost certainly have been baptised as an infant. (Irenaeus of Lyon refers to infant baptism in the second century; it had become near universal in Gaul by the third century, and Patrick's grandfather's being a priest would also suggest his being baptised as an infant.)

xl *Saw in a dream: Conf.* (29) In Latin this section expresses the intimacy of Patrick's relationship to God better than it does in English. The Divine Voice uses the verb *video* (*see* or *view*) and the biblical metaphor we translate as "apple of my eye" to demonstrate that closeness. *Pupilla*, the feminine form of the word used here, means the pupil of the eye.

Pupillus, the masculine form, meaning "fatherless boy" or "orphan," has been employed by Patrick to describe himself, particularly in relation to his Divine Father, Who had assumed the role of guardian or tutor in his regard, a relationship as intimate as that of pupil to eye. Patrick's personal betrayal, the central crisis of his life and of the epistle, revealed God's love for him more than any other. And now the Lord has not only rescued him from the devastation of his "friend's" cruel betrayal, but has elevated Patrick to *the top of the house.*

xli Once the meaning of *designatus* (bishop-elect) is clarified, it renders Leviticus, and indeed the whole epistle much more comprehensible. For more on this subject, see Chapter XIII of *I, Patricius.*

xlii We are now at the very heart of **Leviticus** and of the entire epistle where Patrick expresses his grief for his *dearest friend*, asking two rhetorical questions to which he knows the answers: *Why did we deserve to hear such testimony from him to whom I entrusted my very soul?* and, *But why did it occur to him afterward, in the sight of everyone, good and bad, to dishonor me publicly over something he had freely chosen not to censure, as did the Lord Who is greater than all?*

The answer to the two rhetorical questions occurs between them at the mathematical center of the epistle. Because Latin has no quotation marks, it has been left to translators to insert them. These have been universally misplaced so that elsewhere the sentence reads *"See, you are to be raised to the episcopate" of which I was unworthy.* This reading makes the friend's statement of the obvious (Patrick's elevation, news neither to him nor to his betrayer) the most central and important sentence in the epistle and has Patrick saying: *of which I was unworthy,* something he surely felt, but it is not a confession fit for the drama of the central sentence, especially when the saint's humility is expressed throughout.

Correctly placing the quotation marks after "unworthy" reveals the friend's motive for his betrayal of the saint: envy, and it answers the two parallel questions surrounding it. The betrayer had trouble accepting the fact that he had been passed over for the episcopacy. Without directly accusing his friend, Patrick has corrected the record so that we are able to view the sentence as the most significant of the entire epistle.

Envy was the motivation for holding the hearing when he was absent; for his friend's staging it in hopes of sabotaging Patrick's ordination. To defeat the "friend's" effort Patrick's true friends among "the brethren" rode to Boulogne (or sent a messenger) to inform Patrick of the hearing so he could return in time to defend himself; thus enabling the Irish mission and Patrick's subsequent elevation by the emperor to take place.

We will see in the *Pastoral Epistle* an echo of this construction with the same sin, envy, exposed in the central chiasm of that letter as the motive of another, more serious, betrayal, this time seen by the saint as more directly authored by Satan.

Pride was considered the root of all sin with envy its prime offshoot. Patrick's view of envy is influenced both by the tradition of the Church and by his own experience as expressed in the two epistles we have. Examples of the thinking of early Church Fathers are: "Envy is the congenital malady in human nature"; "Nothing is more opposed to love than envy, and the mother of envy is pride"; "And so it was that man was overcome by the envy of the devil. For that envious and hateful demon, having himself been brought low by his conceit, would not suffer us to attain to the highest things." These thoughts of Sts. Gregory of Nyssa, Augustine and John of Damascus respectively can be found in James R. Payton, Jr. editor. *A Patristic Treasury* (Chesterton: Ancient Faith, 2013) pp. 289, 359, and 455 respectively.

xliii The phrase *neither was I in the Britains* suggests that he had reason to be there since Patrick's statement is directed at those who thought he might have been. Many, believing him to be Romano-British have assumed that Patrick meant that he was with his family, but traditions, both French and

Irish, that he accompanied St. Germanus to Britain to combat Pelagianism, as well as those insisting that he served in Boulogne in the years before going to Ireland, offer other reasons for his presence in the Britains.

What was Patrick doing in Boulogne? He was serving its bishop as deacon before his own elevation to the episcopacy. See Malbrancq, *De Morinis et Morinorum Rebus, tome i* (Tournai: Adrianus Quinque, 1639) 128ff. for references to Patrick's service in Boulogne from 424 until his ordination as bishop in 432. Some have assumed that the saint was bishop at the time, but that could not have been so for many obvious reasons (Church policy, timeline) as well as because Patrick's name was inserted *ad latus*, at the side of the *Catalogue of the Bishops of Boulogne.*

. . . nor was it my idea that he was going to accuse me – in my absence! Patrick uses an interesting verb and construction here for *he was going to accuse me: pulsaret pro me.* This tiny phrase both tells us of the accusation and that his friend would be his defensor.

Pulsare means *to strike, accuse, injure, offend, pound.* But Patrick says his friend is doing these things *pro me, for me, on my behalf!* How succinctly the saint reveals the paradox that his attacker was actually the one appearing to defend him, his *defensor*. For, had there been no such irony, he would have chosen *defendere, tutari*, or *hominis causam dicere,* not *pulsare*.

xliv *"exalt and acknowledge the magnitude of Your being" (exaltarem et magnificarem nomen tuum)* This is often translated *exalt and magnify Your name,* a phrase without resonance for a modern English speaker. It is another example of what is referred to in footnote 24 regarding *Trinity of holiness.* Patrick is not acknowledging the greatness of a word as we understand "name." He is confessing, praising and spreading the good news of God's *holiness*, His *nomen*, His familial, communal being revealed in Christ.

Numbers

xlv **Numbers** is the longest section of the epistle, being the exposition both of the success of Patrick's Irish mission and of his innocence with regard to charges brought against him at his long ago hearing, now revived with his elevation to Patricius. At the same time, it is the saint's glorification of God, to whom he attributes his every success, as well as his deliverance from the consequences of attempts to destroy him.

Throughout **Numbers** Patrick demonstrates the work he has been able to accomplish by God's grace, and defends against the accusation of wishing to enrich himself by going to Ireland raised at his episcopal hearing so many years earlier. **Numbers** is the "proof of the pudding" in which he recounts, not only his numerous successes, but also his many trials and temptations (to accept gifts, to visit his family and brethren in the Church).

The wisdom enabling him to avoid these temptations and remain steadfast in Ireland was not Patrick's. It went against his natural feelings which inclined him to avoid offending those offering gifts and to visit his homeland to see the faces of loved ones.

xlvi *Pupillus*, the word here rendered "orphan" has been universally translated by Patrician scholars as "pupil." The *Apologia* explains why that is not correct for this epistle and why I have used the Latin meaning "fatherless boy" previously. It also means "orphan," which, because he does not mention his mother, may have been his situation early in life. Because, in this case, Patrick had long ago achieved his majority and is more than old enough to have lost both parents, I think "orphan" is meant.

xlvii Mention of sacrifices and humiliations the saint endured is connected to the previous paragraph about his rejection of gifts offered. So far from profiting materially from his Irish mission, what the saint actually gained from the mission is detailed here: loss of his noble status, *outrages from unbelievers*, calumny from his *cognati* in Gaul, persecutions, imprisonment. He is even eager to undergo martyrdom for Christ and His gospel, something that appeared likely to him at the time.

xlviii *Plebs*, here translated as "congregation," in the Late Empire had acquired the definition: "a Christian congregation," which it means in this context. *Plebs, pecora, Scotti, gens, sacerdos* all illustrate the saint's specificity with regard to the words he uses, a specificity we need to respect as we try to understand what he means when he uses them.

xlix *Scotti* is left untranslated in the text to make the same distinction Patrick does. Others translate both *Scotti* and *Hiberniores* as "Irish," but the distinction is meaningful. *Scottus* means "raider." It was a term applied by the Romans to those from Ireland who engaged in that profession and had risen to political dominance by means of it. *Scotti*, as rulers and latecomers to Ireland, were recognized as being distinct from the general population comprised of ethnic groups who had migrated to Ireland earlier, many of whom were now subject to the *Scotti*.

l By Patrick's time there were more than the three parts of Gaul referred to by Julius Caesar, with many subdivisions and an enduring awareness of ethnic and linguistic differences among them. For example, *Lugdunensis* had become the plural *Lugdunenses* with four subdivisions.

Although Latin was the common linguistic bond for the upper classes regardless from which part of Gaul they came, the native population in Belgica II, where Bononia was located, spoke Brythonic while those in *Lugdunenses* spoke the language of the most Gaulish province, the more ancient Goidelic, so that individuals from other parts of Gaul commonly referred to *Lugdunenses* as "the Gauls."

li Now we learn a little more about the elders (*seniores*) in Auxerre who were opposed to Patrick's Irish mission. He doesn't hold their opposition to him against them, understanding that, from their point of view, he lacked the necessary sophistication and experience for such an enterprise. He was as aware as they of the extraordinary nature of his planned extension of the Leinster mission to the pagans of Ulidia. They were almost certainly negatively comparing his qualifications to those of Palladius who was from the most prominent family in Gaul and had been recognized for excelling in his Roman studies. For more on Palladius, see Chapter XI of *I, Patricius.*

lii Patrick, using the elders' worldly yardstick, doubted his own capabilities at the time of his episcopal ordination and failed to comprehend what he now recognizes: God needs neither legal refinements nor worldly sophistication in order to accomplish His ends.

liii The saint is referring to money he spent in order to travel through different *tuatha* and to receive protection. He offers particulars calculated to show that, far from profiting materially from the Irish mission, he spent his own money liberally, careful not to accept gifts from his converts although they were frequently offered.

Deuteronomy

liv *...honor, as yet invisible but believed in the heart:* It is not clear to what Patrick is referring. It may be that some document certifying his elevation had yet to arrive or else he refers to the material rewards he will not receive as a Patricius.

lv The verb *amitto*, here translated as "to let slip away" is elsewhere translated as "to lose," and can mean "send away," "dismiss," "let go." In the present context it is clear that Patrick is unwilling to allow his converts to be lost.

lvi *Ignorantia* is the word translated as *lack of knowledge.* It is a chiastic response to the beginning of the epistle where the saint acknowledges that he is *exceedingly contemptible in the estimation of a great many.* All those considering themselves erudite, possessed of the formal Roman legal education, who were passed over for the episcopate and were never made Patricius, are also among those *cognati* spreading the slanders that threaten the Irish mission by denigrating its founder. Patrick adjusts their focus from the worldly to that of the Kingdom of God.

lvii After this account of God's remarkable interventions in his life, and aware that he is considered ignorant, Patrick humbly implies that perhaps his detractors have themselves been ignorant. They would not have known autobiographical details revelatory of God's action in Patrick's life, but had assumed that Patrick's *ignorantia legi,* or formal ignorance of the law, extended to other areas of learning. One hears echoes of the ancient Roman precept: *"ignorantia juris non excusat"* (ignorance of the law does not excuse) with its implicit suggestion that his detractors' ignorance of Patrick's life and the action of God in it does not excuse their behavior toward him.

Donum Dei means the gift of the Holy Spirit, the pre-eminent "gift of God," as it does in St. John's account of the Samaritan woman at the well (*John 4:4-26*) and in subsequent Christian tradition. The ninth-century western hymn for Pentecost, *Veni Creator Spiritus,* also employs *donum Dei* as a synonym for the Holy Spirit, who comforts, inspires, and bestows wisdom. Patrick is reiterating that what he has accomplished in Ireland is the fruit of Divine Wisdom and neither the byproduct of human effort nor happenstance.

Pastoral Epistle

Part I

lviii Patrick begins this epistle by establishing his authority, offering reasons why he, a well-born Gallo-Roman bishop, is living as an exile among pagans in northeastern Ireland. His position is considered odd to more than his *fratribus et cognatis* and he knows it requires explanation.

It is *for love of God* and *for love of those most dear* [who are] *indeed* [my] *children* that he has chosen to dwell beyond the imperial frontier among those who, because they are not Roman citizens, invite contempt from those who are.

Even before stating that he has been established as a legitimate bishop in Ireland, Patrick gives us his name (also his Roman rank), simultaneously acknowledging himself to be both a sinner and not a man of letters. The latter refers to his lack of the formal legal/literary education received by his fellow bishops in Rome, rather than to education per se, for he is certainly educated.

lix *Proselito et profuga* (a convert and an exile) echoes the *Confessio's proselito et peregrine* (a convert and an alien) near the beginning of **Leviticus**.

lx The saint makes it clear that, far from having contempt for the Irish, (the attitude of many, if not most, Romans toward non-Romans) he considers them "most dear." *Pro dilectione proximorum atque filiorum* has been translated elsewhere *for love of* [my] *nearest neighbors and children* but in this context *proximorum* is better translated, as it often is, figuratively. It is the superlative of *propior* and, when used figuratively, means "most closely related," "most nearly resembling," referring to personal connection or relationship rather than simple physical proximity.

Dilectio is a Late Latin noun for Christian love. Patrick is speaking of those for whom he gave up his former *nearest neighbors* in Gaul and his previous life: the Irish who, through Christian love, have become *those most dear,* [who are] *indeed* [my] *children. Filiorum*, (*sons, children*) in Late Latin has a particular warmth when a clergyman uses it in addressing others. These are the "children" of his spiritual begetting.

lxi ... *even though forsaken by some*, i.e. those who had once been pagans and who apparently have become so again: the apostates. The word here translated (*I am*) *forsaken: contemnor*, from the verb *contemno*, has several definitions and is often rendered by Patrician scholars *I am despised*. In this context, however, an alternative meaning, *forsaken*, is preferable because Patrick is speaking to apostates who have forsaken, not only the faith, but their fellow Christians and their bishop.

That some may despise him personally would not particularly affect Patrick (the saint has previously suffered much more than mere contempt), but everything in this letter conspires to express the deeper suffering that betrayal by apostates in his flock has occasioned: a betrayal of the faith and the Christian community, so much more to be deplored than any personal treachery.

lxii ... *milites: warriors. Milites* is often translated "soldiers" but in this instance we are not dealing with an army or even part of one, so the alternate meaning "warriors" is more appropriate. The men who serve Coroticus are merely fellow outlaws doing his bidding. The conviction that Coroticus was a prince or even a Roman officer, has, I believe, encouraged many to assume that his men were part of some official soldiery when that was certainly not the case.

lxiii The negative comparison the saint makes between God's representative, (himself) and those belonging to the Enemy who have abandoned God, or never knew Him (*murderers bloodied with the blood of innocent Christians*) is directed pointedly at the individual consciences of those once part of his flock. The unspoken question to them is, "With whom do you wish to be allied, these vile scoundrels who are strangers, or those to whom you are kin, not merely by blood, but once, more profoundly, in Christ?"

lxiv If there were any doubt about the status of Coroticus et al., Patrick erases it with his oblique reference to British usurpation (the first line of Part II: *Non usurpo*) and his description here of the Britons' confederates: *associates of Scotti and even of Picts and apostates.*

Some scholars, notably Professor Thomas O'Rahilly in his *Early Irish History and Mythology*, hold that the *Cruithni/ Priteni* (after whom the Pritenic/ Brittanic Isles were named and of whom the Dal n'Araidi were the pre-eminent group in Ulster) were Celts, but not Goidels. I adhere to this opinion as well. But O'Rahilly's assertion that "the Irish Cruithni are never called Picts" is contradicted by investigating a footnote on the same page (342) of his *Early Irish History and Mythology*.

In it he states: "There is no basis for MacNeill's assertion that the Dal n'Araidi are 'named in the Annals both by the Latin name Picti and its Irish equivalent Cruithni or Cruithin.'" In fact, this is misleading, for it is in indices and footnotes that the equivalency is specific and the identification of Dal n'Araidi, Cruithin and Irish Picts, universally recognized. If *a* (Picti) is identical to *b* (Cruithni) and *c* (Dal n'Araidi) is identical to *b* (Cruithni), one realizes that *a* (Picti) and *c* (Dal n'Araidi) are also identical. References can be found in the indices of *The Annals of Ireland by the Four Masters, Annals of Ulster*, and *Annals of Inisfallen*.

Saint Patrick himself calls the Cruithni "Picts" and even O'Rahilly acknowledges that from the third century the Romans called both the Priteni and the Cruithni "Picts," meaning "painted." The saint refers to the only Picts with whom he had any contact, the Cruithni of northeastern Ireland. Since his evangelical labors were conducted primarily among the Ulaid and the Scotti in northeast Ulster, the saint well understood the degradation implicit in reminding the apostates of their close association with Picts.

Because "Picti" was how the Romans referred to the Cruithni, we cannot be surprised that the word does not appear in Irish annals where one expects them to use the Irish word *Cruithni* rather than the Latin.

lxv On the day after the attack, Patrick sent a letter with a trusted priest whom the saint had taught since the man's baptism, along with some other clerics, to plead for the release of the baptised prisoners and of some of the plunder. In response the outlaws laughed scornfully and imprisoned some of the clerics. The words Patrick uses to describe the length of time he knew his priestly emissary are *ab infantia.*

In this instance, *infantia* refers to the priest's baptism or to the time when he began his preparation for orders, rather than to his infancy or childhood, because Patrick the bishop was not occupied in teaching infants but did instruct adults. The priest in question would be in his twenties at the very least, making Patrick's knowledge of him from infancy even less likely. In the Late Empire *infantia* was often used in the former sense or to refer to the period when a person began his clerical or religious education. See Lanigan, *op. cit Vol. I,* 300, n. 104.

lxvi The two groups for whom Patrick *weeps* are the victims and the apostates: *those whom the Devil has so thoroughly ensnared.* Although he claims not to know for whom he should weep more, this is a rhetorical statement. It is obvious from what follows that he is most concerned about those former converts whose eternal salvation was in jeopardy, who have become *strangers to me and to Christ, my God.* For the murdered and kidnapped Christians, fresh from the purifying waters of baptism, will enjoy eternal life even though their entrance into it was needlessly violent.

lxvii *Parricide! Fratricide!* It is possible that during the raid the father(s) and brother(s) of one or more of the newly-baptized Christians may have been killed. Otherwise "brother" must be understood as meaning "brother in Christ." Perhaps an older man who had led an individual to the faith might be considered a "father in Christ" but nothing in the epistle makes such distinctions. Rather the saint's audience is simply being led to consider their kinship with those who have been murdered, regardless of whether that relationship was one of flesh or spirit. For close kinship greatly magnifies a crime, particularly among the Irish who placed the highest premium on kinship.

Part II

lxviii *I do not exceed my authority,* begins Patrick, *Non usurpo.* The Latin word *usurpo* is a pointed reference to the fact that Coroticus' relatives and other tyrants in Britain, *did* usurp to gain the positions they occupy. Native British "tyrants" forcibly took control of their localities when Roman officials left with the military in the early years of the fifth century.

The tyrants and Coroticus himself have only the spurious authority they granted themselves, while Patrick's authority has been bestowed by God through bishops of the Church, recently reinforced by the Roman emperor's formal recognition of his accomplishments. Late Latin adds *presume* to earlier definitions of *usurpo*, which is why it has been translated here as *I do not presume to exceed my authority* rather than *I am not usurping authority.*

After drawing this distinction between himself and Coroticus, Patrick reminds his audience of what lends weight to his words before resuming his attack on his real adversary, Satan. He follows that attack with appeals to his flock, which, in his mind, still includes those who have abandoned it.

He exercises authority in two ways: first, by interpreting God's law and preaching the gospel, and second, by binding and loosing. Patrick is not attempting to reach *Coroticus, who reveres neither God nor His chosen priests,* with arguments that only make sense to Christians, or with personal appeals only affecting for those who once had loved and followed him.

lxix The saint warns *the holy and humble of heart,* not to flatter or associate with the outlaws until the latter do sufficient penance. If there are those listening to him who have not actually participated in the raid, yet are tempted to receive some of the plunder or to re-admit unrepentant apostates into their circle of friendship, Patrick declares them to be as culpable as the perpetrators. He will return to this theme again in Part III, refining the point he is making: *God will judge. For it is written: "Not only those who commit evil deeds, but also those who agree with them, will be condemned."*

lxx . . . *et liberent servos Dei et ancillas Xristi baptizatas* . . . The distinction made between *the servants of God* and *the baptised handmaidens of Christ* must mean that some of the clerics sent with Patrick's initial letter were captured; not all, because at least one returned with the information that the criminals *laughed scornfully* and that the others had been retained.

It implies that Coroticus' henchmen did not abduct any newly baptised men, just women who were more easily overcome. The former would have been those *brutally massacred, slain by the swords of the previously mentioned men.*

lxxi *The Most High rejects gifts from the unjust . . .* Apparently some apostates entertained the delusion that they could make an offering that would appease God for things they had stolen – while they kept the rest. The violence of the quotes Patrick chose to illustrate their fate, if they did not repent and make restitution, should have left no doubt in their minds about the consequences should they remain obdurate.

lxxii The final paragraph of Part II accuses the apostates of murder even if they themselves did not perform any killings. They have "hated" their brethren in consorting with those who did perform the crimes, thus they too are murderers, not merely traitors and avaricious thieves. Nor were these ordinary murders of godless individuals like the Britons, but of *children of God whom He recently procured from the farthest corners of the earth,* persons to whom they were related by blood and, previously, by grace.

Part III

lxxiii Part III begins with questions Patrick immediately answers, explaining that he has severed his familial bonds at the prompting of the Holy Spirit. He follows this by asking a related question: *Is it from myself that I have religious compassion for that pagan people who captured me and ravaged the servants and handmaidens of my father's house?* From where did this sacrificial impulse come? From himself? Hardly. Nothing natural would inspire a person to leave everything a human being holds dear in order to return to barbarians who had previously forced him at an early age to do so against his will and had enslaved him for six years.

Then, to emphasize just how great was the sacrifice he had made, and thus, how great the love inspiring it, Patrick reveals enough of his background to show that he not only had left loved ones, but he also had abandoned an elevated position as an aristocratic Roman citizen in order to employ his wealth on behalf of the very people who had previously kidnapped him *and ravaged the servants and handmaidens of my father's house.*

All of this argumentation is to demonstrate that his coming to Ireland was contrary to earthly calculations. It was prompted solely by love of God, and of the Irish, to serve whom he left everything humans hold dear. Do we hear an echo of his insistence in **Deuteronomy** of the *Confessio: ... I have never had reasons other than the gospel and its promises for going back to that pagan people from whom I barely escaped before*?

lxxiv At the beginning of Part II Patrick had said . . . *etsi invidet inimicus per tyrannidem Corotici* (6): . . . *despite the Enemy's envy* [expressed] *through the tyranny of Coroticus,* which introduces the idea that his success in winning souls has stirred up Satan's envy for which Coroticus is merely a conduit.

Part III returns to this theme with the simple statement: *Invidetur mihi. (I am envied.)* following it with a brief prayer beginning, *What shall I do, Lord?* that draws his listeners with him into his own constant awareness of the presence of God. The exact center of the *Confessio* reveals that the sin of envy was the catalyst for Patrick's personal betrayal, the worst, most humiliating experience of his life up to that time. Similarly, at the very center of the *Pastoral Epistle* we find the same sin behind the attack on Patrick's new converts, an even more profound betrayal and suffering.

The *Confessio* credits Patrick's "success" in having been made a bishop with arousing envy in the heart of his closest friend who had been passed over as unworthy of the episcopacy. Here Patrick appears to view Coroticus' attack as analogous. In this case it is the saint's success in converting pagans to Christ that is seen as the catalyst for the envy of God unleashed by the Enemy and manifested through his puppets: Coroticus and confederates.

lxxv The negative comparison Patrick makes of British raiders with the Franks betrays Patrick's Gallic origins for, were he from Britain, such an analogy would have been foreign to him. If indeed he were British, he would have been better served by an analogy closer to home, one with which he, his hearers, and their leader, were all familiar. But Patrick possessed no equivalent British analogy because his background was not British.

In this instance, Patrick aims directly at the Britons since they have the power to release the captives and make restitution. He reduces Britons, who may even be Roman citizens, to a level below non-Roman pagan Franks, with whom one could at least bargain to prevent the killing or selling of Christian captives.

lxxvi The seriousness of the crimes committed and their eternal consequences have been vividly delineated. Now the saint mourns, not just on behalf of himself and the bereaved families, but on behalf of the entire Church. His grief, crescendoing to the intensity of a howl (or an Irish *caoin*), is followed immediately by confession of his powerlessness to do more than speak to the hearts of his hearers.

lxxvii This sentence adds to the evidence (his poverty, the numbers dedicating themselves to religious life) that the *Pastoral Epistle* was composed close in time to the *Confessio* because both epistles were written after his elevation to Patricius and, because towards the end of his life, he expresses the same physical limitations, the same poverty.

I am able to come neither to the assistance of God nor men. (16) *Dignus*, often translated as "worthy," also means "fit," "suitable," "convenient." It is here translated as "able" because I believe that is Patrick's meaning in context. He is not fit enough, not suitable, in the sense of "able." In his present state of old age, poverty, and ill health, he is physically incapable of coming to the aid of the victims. Surely, after all his years of serving God and man, questions of *worthiness* would not prevent the saint from assisting now – if he were physically and financially able – since they had never stopped him before.

lxxviii The saint is saying that *unjust men* consider it inappropriate, somehow *dishonorable, that we are Irish.* In this case, *we are* means *I am*, but it is an *I* inseparably united to the rest of the Irish. To some, Patrick's self-identification with the Irish is shameful, because they would view union with a non-Roman pagan people as stooping from the high estate of Roman citizenship to a figurative status of non-citizen.

It was not unsuitable for the Irish to be what they were, yet some felt it unsuitable for a Gallo-Roman to identify himself as Irish, who, being outside Roman frontiers, were deemed contemptible by those within them. Patrick demonstrates his willingness to suffer that contempt with the Irish as one of them.

Part IV

lxxix As in the last section of the *Confessio*, Patrick soars spiritually when he comes to Part IV, the finale of this epistle. Here once again, with even more passionate imagery, he contrasts the future of the victims with that of their captors. And, as before, his primary audience is the apostates.

Grief has become prayer, ostensibly for all the outlaws involved in the raid, but actually for the only portion of that group he could hope to reach – those who understand the faith-based arguments he presents: the apostates. All the sin and horror of the devastating raid are swallowed up in the saint's overwhelming love for God and man and his hope for the salvation of even the deluded, greedy apostates.

lxxx [They] *will perish from the presence of the Lord* in Latin is: *a facie Domini peribunt.* The critical word is *facie*, often translated as "face." But the word also means the true form of something as opposed to its image. In this case we are speaking of eternity and banishment from the vision of God as He may be known by those who love Him.

lxxxi *Imperitia*, the word translated as *imperfect knowledge* might actually be a Late Latin word *inperitia* meaning lack of religious knowledge. Without being able to study the manuscripts themselves, or knowing what changes might have been made to the calligraphy in transmission, it is impossible to know. But the context, which is of specifically religious knowledge, suggests that the original word may indeed have been *inperitia*.

lxxxii The whole *Pastoral Epistle* is distilled in Patrick's final prayer that God will inspire the lost sheep *to return to their senses and repent;* that they will *free the baptised women whom they have captured so that they may deserve to live for God and be made whole both here and in eternity.*

lxxxiii Patrick's last words are a blessing. Translating them was difficult because Christians are used to hearing "In the name of the Father and of the Son and of the Holy Spirit" and, at first glance Patrick's words appear to say "Peace to (or 'for') the Father and of the Son and of the Holy Spirit." The three nouns are in the dative case (to or for), but it just doesn't seem right until one remembers that "for" is not just giving, but can mean "on behalf of." The latter is the only way I can make sense of the blessing because one does not presume to offer peace to the Author of it.

Lorica

lxxxiv This poem is inspired by a hymn based on the *Lorica,* a poetic prayer attributed to St. Patrick, but not earlier than the eighth century. Regardless of when or by whom it was written, the prayer is expressive of the soul of the man who evangelized Ireland and wrote these epistles.

Chronology

lxxxv The entries were made long after the date and must be related to these 443 entries: "Patricius, the bishop, flourishing in the zeal of faith and the doctrine of Christ in our Province." (AU) and *"Patricius in Christi doctrina floruit."* (AI) The latter source seems to have derived its information from the former. Leo, bishop of Rome, attempted to extend his jurisdiction beyond his own diocese, laying a foundation for the western papacy and the East-West schism six centuries later. *Probatus est* meant that a bishop was free from heresy, most particularly Pelagianism. It is unclear whether these entries refer to an actual incident or reflect a much later situation vis a vis Roman papal power, interpolated into the period of Patrick's life.

Select References

Barley, M.W. and Hanson, R. P. C., eds. *Christianity in Britain: 300-700* (Leicester: University of Leicester, 1968)

Bertrand, Pierre Jean Baptiste. *Precis de l'Histoire Physique, Politique, et Civile de la Ville de Boulogne-sur-mer et de ses Environs* (Boulogne: J. Le Roy, 1828)

Bieler, Ludwig. *Codices Patriciani Latini: a descriptive catalogue of Latin manuscripts relating to St. Patrick* (Dublin: Dublin Institute for Advanced Studies 1942)

Libri Epistolarum Sancti Patricii Episcopi, 2 vols. (Dublin: Dublin Stationery Office 1952)

The Works of St. Patrick. St. Secundinus Hymn on St. Patrick (London and Maryland: The Newman Press, 1953)

"Vindicianae Patricianae: Remarks on the Present State of Patrician Studies" in *Irish Ecclesiastical Record,* Series 5, Vol 79 (Dublin: Browne and Nolan, 1953) 161-85

"A Linguist's View of St. Patrick: Remarks on a Recent Study of St. Patrick's Latinity" in *Eigse 10* (Dublin: National University of Ireland, 1961-62) 149-52

The Patrician Texts in the Book of Armagh (Dublin: Dublin Institute for Advanced Studies, 1979)

Bingham, Joseph. *Origines Ecclesiasticae: The Antiquities of the Christian Church* (London: Robert Knaplock, 1846)

Birley, Anthony. *Life in Roman Britain,* 5th imprint (London: Batsford, 1977)

Borius, Rene, trans. *Constance de Lyon: Vie de St Germain d'Auxerre* in *Sources Chretiennes 112* (Paris: Editions du Cerf, 1965)

Bucherius, Aegidius. *Belgium Romanum Ecclesiasticum et Civile* (Tournai: Hovius, 1655)

Bullet, Jean-Baptiste. *Memoires sur la Langue Celtique,* tome III (Lyon: Claude-Joseph Daclin for l'Academie des Sciences, 1754)

Bury, Rev. John Bagnall. *The Life of Saint Patrick and His Place in History* (London: Macmillan & Co., 1905)

Clancy, Thomas Owen. *"The Real St. Ninian" in The Innes Review,* Vol. 52, no. 1 (Edinburgh: Edinburgh University Press, 2001) 1-28

Dinneen, Rev. Patrick M.A., D.Litt., compiler and ed. *A Smaller Irish-English Dictionary* (Dublin: Gill & Son, 1923)

Dottin, Georges. *La Langue Gaulois* (Paris: C. Clincksieck, 1920)

Egan, Patricia Colling. *I, Patricius: The Roman History of an Irish Saint* (Maysville, MO: St. Nicholas Press, 2021)

Fleming, Rev. William Canon. *Boulogne-sur-Mer, St. Patrick's Native Town* (Los Angeles: Hardpress Publishing, 2016 [1907])

Gougaud, Dom Louis. *Christianity in Celtic Lands* (Blackrock: Four Courts Press, 1995 [1932])

Grandgent, Charles Hall. *An Introduction to Vulgar Latin.* (Boston: D.C. Heath & Co., 1907)

Grosjean, Paul. "Analyse du Livre d'Armagh," *Analecta Bollandiana* (Brussels: Societe des Bollandistes, 1944) 33- 41

"S. Patrice a Auxerre sous S. Germain," *Analecta Bollandiana* 75 (Brussels: Societe des Bollandistes, 1957) 158-174

Gwynn, John. *Liber Ardmachanus: The Book of Armagh* (Dublin: Hodges, Figgis & Co., 1913)

Haddan, Arthur West and Stubbs, William, eds. *Council and Ecclesiastical Documents Relating to Great Britain and Ireland* V. 1 (Oxford: Clarendon Press, 1869)

Hanson, R.P.C. *St. Patrick: His Origins and His Career* (Oxford: Clarendon Press, 1968)

"The D-Text of Patrick's Confession: Original or Reduction?" in *PRIA 77C* (Dublin: Royal Irish Academy, 1977) 251-256

Harbison, Peter. *Pre-Christian Ireland* (London: Thames and Hudson, 1988)

Howlett, David. *The Book of Letters of Saint Patrick the Bishop* (Blackrock: Four Courts Press, 1994)

Muirchu Moccu Mactheni's 'Vita Sancti Patricii' (Blackrock: Four Courts Press, 2006)

Hogan, Edmund S.J. *Onomasticon Goedelicum* (Blackrock: Four Courts Press, 1993)

Johnson, Stephen. *Later Roman Britain* (London: Routledge and Kegan Paul, 1980)

Keating, Rev. Geoffrey D.D. *Foras Feasa ar Eirinn,* trans. by John O'Mahoney as *The History of Ireland* (New York: P.M. Haverty, 1857 [c.1632])

Kelly, Joseph. "The Escape of Saint Patrick from Ireland" *Studia Patristica* XVIII (Leuven: Peeters Publishers,1983) 41-45

Kenney, James. *Sources for the Early History of Ireland,* Revised ed. (Blackrock: Four Courts Press, 1993 [1929])

Lanigan, Rev. John D.D. *An Ecclesiastical History of Ireland,* 4 Vols. (Dublin: Graisberry, 1822)

Leverett, F.P., ed. *A New and Copious Lexicon of the Latin Language: compiled chiefly from the Magnum Totius Latinitatis Lexicon of Facciolati and Forcellini, and the German Works of Scheller and Luenemann* (Boston: Rice and Kendall, 1853)

Lodge, R. Anthony. "The Latinisation of Gaul" in *French: From Dialect to Standard* (London, New York: Routledge, 1993) 29-53

Mackenzie, Lord Thomas. *Studies in Roman Law, with comparative views of the laws of France, England and Scotland* (Edinburgh: W. Blackwood, 1865)

MacNeill, Eoin. "The Native Place of St. Patrick" in *Proceedings of the Royal Irish Academy* XXXVII (Dublin: Royal Irish Academy, 1926) 118-140

Mac Niocaill, Gearoid. *Ireland Before the Vikings.* (Dublin: Gill and Macmillan, 1972)

Malbrancq, Jacobus. *De Morinis et Morinorum Rebus,* 3 Vols. (Tournai: Adrianus Quinque, 1639-1654)

Meriaux, Charles. "Therouanne et son diocese jusqu'a la fin de l'epoque Carolingienne" in *Bibliotheque de l'Ecole des chartes* (Dialnet: 2000) 377-406

Mohrmann, Christine. *The Latin of St. Patrick* (Dublin: Dublin Institute for Advanced Studies, 1961)

Etudes sur le latin des Chretiens, Tome IV: Latin chretien et latin medieval (Rome: Edizioni di storia e letteratura, 1977)

Notitia Dignitatum and ***Notitia Galliarum*** (c. 395) See www.bnf.fr or http://gallica.bnf.fr. (c. 395-400)

O'Donovan, John Ll.D., M.R.I.A. *A Grammar of the Irish Language* (Dublin: Hodges and Smith: 1845)

ed. *The Four Masters Annals of the Kingdom of Ireland: from the earliest times to the year 1616,* 7 Vols., 3rd Edition (Blackrock: Edmund Burke Publisher, 1998/1851)

O Muraile, Nollaig, ed. *Annala Uladh: The Annals of Ulster* (Blackrock: Edmund Burke Publisher, 1998/1887)

O'Reilly, Edward. *O'Reilly's Irish-English Dictionary with a Supplement by John O'Donovan, LL.D., M.R.I.A.* (Dublin: James Duffy & Sons, 1864 [1817])

O'Rahilly, Thomas F. "Review of L. Bieler, *The Life and Legend of St.Patrick,*" in *IHS* 8 (Cambridge: Cambridge University Press, 1952-53) 268-279

Early Irish History and Mythology (Dublin: Dublin Institute for Advanced Studies: 1984/1946)

Rocque, John. *A Map of the Kingdom of Ireland* (London: Laurie and Whittle, 1794)

de Rosny, J. Hector. *Histoire du Boulonnais,* t. I (Amiens: Imprimerie Yvert, 1868)

de Rosny, M.E. *Memoires de la Societe Academique de l'Arondissement de Boulogne sur Mer,* t.10 (Boulogne: Simonnaire & Cie., 1879)

Roymans, Nico, ed. *From the Sword to the Plough: Three Studies in the early Romanisation of Gaul* (Amsterdam: Amsterdam Archaeological Studies, 1996)

Ryan, Rev. John, SJ., ed. *Saint Patrick: Radio Eireann Thomas Davis Lectures* (Dublin: Dublin Stationery Office, 1958)

"A Difficult Phrase in the 'Confession' of St. Patrick" in *Irish Ecclesiastical Record* (Dublin: Browne and Nolan, 1938) 299

Seiller, Claude. "Le castrum et le port de Gesoriacum (Boulogne-sur-Mer). Base de la Classis Britannica (IIe-IIIe siecles)" in *Archaeology in Confrontation* (Ghent: Academia Press, 1984) 201-211

"La presence militaire a Boulogne-sur-Mer (F.) au Bas-Empire" in Lodewijckx, M., ed. *Archaeological and Historical Aspects of West-European Societies* (Leuven: Leuven University Press, 1996)

Simpson, D.P. *Cassell's Latin Dictionary* (New York: Macmillan Publishing, 1977)

Smith, William and Cheetham, Samuel. *A Dictionary of Christian Antiquities,* Vol. I (London: John Murray, 1875)

Souter, Alexander, compiler. *A Glossary of Later Latin to 600 A.D.* (Oxford: Clarendon Press, 1996)

Thomas, Charles. *The Early Christian Archaeology of North Britain* (Oxford: Oxford University Press, 1971)

Christianity in Roman Britain to AD 500 (Los Angeles: University of California Press, 1981)

Thompson, E. A. *St. Germanus of Auxerre and the End of Roman Britain* (Woodbridge, Suffolk: The Boydell Press, 1988)

Who was St. Patrick? (Suffolk: The Boydell Press, 1999)

Vacant, A., Mangenot, E., and Amann, E., eds. *Dictionnaire de Theologie Catho-lique* (Paris: Editions Letouzet et Ane, 1899-1950)

Vaillant, Victor Jules. *Epigraphie de Morinie ou inscriptions gallo-romaines sur pierre, metal etc.* (Boulogne-sur-mer: Simonnaires & Cie., 1890)

Wacher, John S. *The Towns of Roman Britain* (London: Routledge, 1997)

White, N.J.D., ed. 1905 "Libri Sancti Patricii – the Latin writings of Saint Patrick" 201-306 in *Proceedings of the Royal Irish Academy*, Vol. 25, Section C (Dublin: Royal Irish Academy, 1905) 201-306

Wightman, Edith Mary. *Gallia Belgica* (Berkeley: University of California Press, 1985)

Williams, Hugh. *Christianity in Early Britain* (Oxford: Clarendon Press, 1912)

Winterbottom, Michael. *Gildas: The Ruin of Britain and Other Works* (London: Phillimore, 1978)

Yonge, Charles Duke, trans. *The Roman History of Ammianus Marcellinus* (London: Bell & Sons, 1911)